The Life & Impact of Phil Parshall

ENDORSEMENTS

This volume is a fitting tribute to Phil and Julie Parshall. Not only do the contributors demonstrate the global impact of Parshall's writings, but they also build on his work in a variety of ways—engaging in biblical theology and sociological analysis, refining methodology and metrics. The need for Christians to bring the gospel to Muslims has never been greater. These contributors connect a new generation of missionaries with Parshall's work, inspiring further commitment to thoughtful witness.

CARMEN JOY IMES
professor of Old Testament at Prairie College
author, *Bearing God's Name: Why Sinai Still Matters*

I'm jealous … I wanted to write a whole biography of Phil and Julie Parshall, and I earnestly hope somebody does. For now, may *The Life and Impact of Phil Parshall* not merely inspire readers to emulate Phil, who has challenged us to constantly keep on asking, "How can we do it better, wiser, and deeper?" but also move many to take up persevering residence among the most neglected, suffering Muslims on earth … through wars, famine, and floods, even denying themselves the joy of a large family to be more available to those whose families are in danger of being lost for eternity. Thank you, Phil, and Julie, for your contagious example both in thinking and doing.

GREG LIVINGSTONE
founder, Frontiers

Christians with a heart for communicating the gospel of Jesus Christ effectively in cross-cultural contexts cannot afford to neglect the conversation in which the experienced missiologists of this book invite their readers' thoughtful participation. The decades of experience each of the seven contributors, together with the mentor they honor in this volume, Phil Parshall, reflects the investment of extensive time and treasure within various cultures of Islam. The principles they endeavor to refine here will sharpen the approach and better the wisdom of everyone who recognizes the challenge—in cross-cultural mission among any people group—of unburdening the gospel of the assumptions of one's own culture in bringing it to another. Still, for all its thought-provoking analysis, the book offers the reader no mere technical manual. Its pages are inspired by the love each author has for the Muslims with whom they share life and by the desire each one has that these beloved people would one day also share in the atoning power of Jesus.

DONALD WESTBLADE
professor of religion, Hillsdale College

Topics related to Muslim followers of Jesus are hotly debated in missiology today. Phil Parshall, through his humble and gentle spirit and forty years as an effective cross-cultural witness among Muslims, has been an innovative pioneer in Muslim evangelism, opening the door for new ways of thinking, relating to, and living among Muslims. Others have built on his foundational principles and at times taken his contextualization ideas beyond his theological comfort zone. Now seven missiologists have written captivating, helpful, and practical essays to honor Phil Parshall. What a great gift they have given to missiologists and mission practitioners today.

DARRELL WHITEMAN
Global Development, Inc.

This book reflects and builds on the insights of Phil Parshall, a contemporary leader in Christian mission among Muslims, with whom I have had the privilege of working in the classroom and the mission field for many years. Likewise, the contributors bring a similar blend of the academy, experience, and creative insight. This book should be on the short list of every missionary to Muslims who wishes to enrich his or her call with the insights of those in whose footsteps they are privileged to walk.

J. DUDLEY WOODBERRY
dean emeritus and senior professor of Islamic Studies, Fuller Theological Seminary

The Life & Impact of Phil Parshall

Connecting with Muslims

KENNETH NEHRBASS
AND MARK WILLIAMS,
EDITORS

WILLIAM
CAREY
PUBLISHING
Available at missionbooks.org

Published by William Carey Publishing
10 W. Dry Creek Cir
Littleton, CO 80120 | www.missionbooks.org

William Carey Publishing is a ministry of Frontier Ventures
Pasadena, CA 91104 | www.frontierventures.org

Cover and Interior Designer: Mike Riester
Copyeditor: Andy Sloan
Managing Editor: Melissa Hicks

Cover photo courtesy of Dr. Jim Plueddemann

ISBNs: 978-1-64508-336-8 (paperback)
        978-1-64508-338-2 (mobi)
        978-1-64508-339-9 (epub)

Printed Worldwide

25 24 23 22 21   1 2 3 4 5   IN

Library of Congress Control Number: 2021938071

For Phil and Julie Parshall

In memory of Mark Williams

CONTENTS

PREFACE
Mark S. Williams

Why would you want to read a book inspired by the life and work of a missionary who worked for four decades with Muslims? If you're working in Islamic contexts right now, you're probably familiar with Phil Parshall's contributions. But what if you've never heard of Dr. Parshall, or never met a Muslim? It turns out that Parshall's conviction that culture matters—that the gospel should make sense in local contexts—is as true for North Americans as it is for sub-Saharan Africans or East Asians. Looking back, I realize my own journey toward Christ was made possible because people worshiped God in ways that were relevant to my own cultural setting in Southern California.

As I was entering my junior year of high school, I had two good friends—one was a Roman Catholic ("charismatic Catholic") and the other was a Lutheran. At that time, I was the product of a nominal Christian (Episcopalian) home. But both of these friends were talking to me about having a vibrant faith in Jesus—something that was not a part of my "Christian" experience at that time.

After some weeks, my Lutheran friend invited me to his church's youth group—just to see how I would like it. I really did like it; and I joined that church soon afterwards. This friend also told me about radio station KYMS, 106.3 FM, where I was introduced to pop and rock music that was "Christian." Until then, I had no idea there even was "Christian pop" and "Christian rock" music!

Finally, this friend took me to a Saturday night concert at a different kind of church in Costa Mesa, California. At Calvary Chapel, headed by Pastor Chuck Smith, I heard in person the Christian bands that I had been listening to on KYMS. Instead of traditional hymns, a band played Christian worship songs with pop and rock styles. Calvary Chapel was already developing Maranatha Music; and the rise of a contextualized style of worship and form of church—attractive to young teens like me—was born.[1]

---

1 Almost immediately, I became enamored with Pastor Chuck Smith's "C3" Christ-centered community—called Calvary Chapel. See my article "Revisiting the C1-C6 Spectrum in Muslim Contextualization," *Missiology* 39, no. 3 (2011): 337.

After being married in 1985, my wife and I prayed about serving in China, as we felt that we were called there. A few years later we sought out a mission agency that was symbiotically related to the Bible school we both attended. When we went through their candidate orientation, they informed us that there was no placement on mainland China at that time (the year was 1989— the year of the Tiananmen Square incident).

The personnel director of the mission agency went on to say, "There is, however, in the country of the Philippines, an exciting collaboration between SIM, OMF, and SEND. SEND is a mission consortium that was created with the intention of reaching the Magindanaon people—the largest Muslim people group of the southern Philippines on the island of Mindanao. Our agency sends missionaries to SIM for this work. The one in charge of this consortium is Dr. Phil Parshall, a leading innovator in the principles of contextualization in Muslim ministry. Before deciding whether or not to join this consortium, it is advisable to read Dr. Parshall's book, *New Paths in Muslim Evangelism*, and to take courses through the Zwemer Institute of Muslim Studies near Fuller Seminary in Pasadena, California."

This is the context in which I want to introduce to you my long-time friend and mentor (to many others, as well as to me) in ministry to Muslims, Phil Parshall (DMiss, Fuller Seminary). As my wife and I joined Serving in Mission (SIM) in that ministry context in April 1990, we embarked on a thirty-plus-year journey with "evangelical contextualization" theory and practice—mostly in the realm of Muslim contexts. With the highest esteem for my dear friend Phil Parshall, I count it a great privilege to write the preface to this *Festschrift*[2] in honor of "Kuya Phil" (Brother Phil), as he is known to like-minded Filipino missionaries in the Philippines.

While Phil is arguably best known for his writings on contextualization strategies in Muslim contexts, one of my favorite writings is his ponderings on keeping missionaries "safe" in their ministry allocations, addressed in his 1994 *Evangelical Missions Quarterly* article "Missionaries: Safe or Expendable?" That hard-hitting commentary will likely continue to stimulate thinking and conversation, even in the context of recent evacuations due to world events like COVID-19.

The list of articles that Phil has written for *EMQ*, *Christianity Today*, and *Missiology* constitute a substantial bibliography in and of itself (see the appendix). His contribution to evangelical missiology is rounded out nicely by nearly one dozen monographs and books he has written on topics of evangelism and mission to Muslims over the course of a missionary career

2 *Festschrift* is a German term defined by Webster's as "a volume of writings by different authors presented as a tribute or memorial especially to a scholar."

that spanned from 1962 to 2006. In addition to *The Cross and the Crescent* (Tyndale, 1989), Phil's more prolific publications from Baker Book House include *New Paths in Muslim Evangelism* (1980), *Bridges to Islam* (1983), and *Inside the Community* (1994).

It is for this servant of God, then, that the contributors to this Festschrift offer their musings on various topics related to ministry to Muslims, evangelical contextualization, and broader concerns of missiology—put forward in a thought-provoking style similar to that of our brother and colleague in mission, Phil. Indeed, he would welcome the discussions brought forward in this volume as per his statement in his *EMQ* article "Danger! New Directions in Contextualization," written in 1998: "Let's bring the subject out in the open and dialogue together" (410).

Phil and Julie Parshall, courtesy of Phil and Julie Parshall

INTRODUCTION
Kenneth Nehrbass

Whether or not you work with Muslims, this book will inspire you to respect the culture of the Other. It will help you think through what contextualization looks like in an age of globalization. Christian outreach among resistant groups can be discouraging; but the contributors to this book have encouraging stories to tell about the progress that can be made when you make friends across cultures by learning from them, and even serving them.

In chapter 1, Gary R. Corwin summarizes the life and legacy of Phil Parshall. In some ways, Phil's formative Christian journey was rather unremarkable: He was raised in the church; he had a personal awakening; after some pursuing, he persuaded his sweetheart to marry him; and then he went to Bible college. Yet in other ways, Parshall's ministry and influence has been extraordinary: He pioneered the field of Muslim contextualization through his twelve academic books and many articles (see the appendix). Parshall inspired Corwin, along with most of the contributors in this book (and countless other missionaries), to learn and respect the cultures of Muslims, and to pass on what they learned to others.

Parshall's ideas about missions among Muslims were innovative. Yet sometimes thinking outside of the box can put you in a lonely place. In chapter 2, Kevin Higgins develops a metaphor of innovations in folk music to describe how Parshall's creative approaches to missions were subsequently misunderstood by critics and adopted by fans. Higgins is one of these fans who took Parshall's ideas in a slightly different direction as he speaks of "holy envy" and finds ways that indigenous "forms" can be kept if they serve a Christian "function."

In chapter 3, Miriam Adeney describes the "sacrifices" Parshall was willing to make (like giving up pork) in order to live at peace with Muslims. Ethnic culture matters to people, and even in an age of globalization we all still find identity in our cultural roots. Adeney looks at the book of Acts to explore how cultural differences were meted out by the early church. She suggests that the task of contextualization today is the same as that of the early church, and of Parshall: The church must reflect local cultures, but we cannot dilute the gospel.

In chapter 4, Enoch Jinsik Kim depicts the fuzzy zone in which many Muslim background believers negotiate their multiple identities. Contemporary Muslims in urban centers behave appropriately in the mosque but need to draw on different aspects of their identity at work, or at other social settings. Kim observes that evangelism in such a complex context cannot be as simple as Western faith development models often suggest. Perhaps we need to encourage the multiple "memberships" held by Muslim background believers (MBBs).

Harley Talman, in chapter 5, addresses three barriers to discipling Muslims: differences in cultural identity, religious identity, and communal identity. He suggests ways to smooth out these obstacles to conversion. Here Talman relates an incredibly successful case study of evangelism in a Muslim setting.

In chapter 6, Joseph S. Williams asks whether the C1-6 spectrum is prescriptive or descriptive. The spectrum aims to help Muslim background believers (MBBs) avoid syncretism, but it also aims to help Christianity feel familiar, rather than foreign, to MBBs. Williams recognizes that in an age of globalization, MBBs may naturally balance cultural maintenance, on the one hand, with their identification with the global church on the other hand. Additionally, culture and religion are inextricably linked: What looks like a religious convention to outsiders (e.g., the religious moniker "Muslim," or submitting by wearing *hijab*) may be perceived as a cultural convention—not a religious one—by insiders. Because of the specific nuances of religious and cultural identities in various contexts, it may be impossible for outsiders to prescribe the "best" space on the spectrum for Muslim background believers to inhabit. In fact, Williams points out, syncretism can be found at virtually every stage on the spectrum; and biblically grounded Christians can also be found across the C1-6 spectrum.

Last, we look at John Jay Travis's encouraging thoughts based on his years of living among Muslims in South and Southeast Asia. He reflects on how he, along with his family and coworkers, developed meaningful cross-cultural relationships—applying many of Parshall's suggestions on lifestyle, religious vocabulary, hospitality, spirituality, and cultural bonding.

Mark Williams, a longtime colleague of the Parshalls, conceived this book. He asked me to serve essentially as a midwife—to make sure the project is healthy and sees the light of day. Tragically, Mark passed away suddenly on June 29, 2020. Before his passing, he was able to read most of the chapters presented here. He told me he was thrilled both by the original insights into contextualization and by the way the book honors Phil Parshall. I'm confident that the book will teach you a bit about Phil Parshall, and even inspire you to read some of his works. I also believe the book will encourage you to press ahead on the paths of contextualized outreach to the lost.

1
THE LIFE AND LEGACY OF PHIL PARSHALL

Gary R. Corwin

Dr. Phil Parshall is to contextualization among Muslims what Thomas Edison was to the utilization of electricity. Phil hasn't been afraid to experiment, but he has always done so while respecting where the real power lies: in the power of God and the gospel to bring about change in the most recalcitrant sinner. He has always recognized, and has also warned others, of the great danger in mishandling that power in the process of communicating the gospel.

Speaking of Thomas Edison, it is interesting to note that Parshall's paternal grandfather, a modestly successful welder/businessman, often spoke proudly of doing work for Edison when he spent winters near their home in Fort Myers, Florida. Parshall notes in his memoir that his "grandmother derived even greater joy relating her stories about playing bridge with Mrs. Edison."[1]

It must be acknowledged here at the outset that Phil Parshall and his dear wife, Julie, are to me not only subjects to be researched and written about, but dear friends of many decades. I will do my best to be objective, but I feel obliged to warn the reader upfront.

Sources required to adequately address the life and legacy of Phil Parshall must obviously include the usual ones that illuminate his formative years, his ministry labors in two very different contexts, and his substantial literary output. But there must also be those sources that show the relational connections that influenced his views, that spread and built on his insights, and that significantly influenced the organizations with which he has been associated. It is beyond the scope of this chapter to address all that, but it is likely that the reader will discover many of the relational connections related to Parshall's views addressed in this and other chapters in this book. This chapter, however, will focus more narrowly on his life and work, gleaned primarily from his memoir *Divine Threads*. It will conclude with my assessment of Parshall's impact missiologically and personally in the lives of others.

---

1 Parshall, *Divine Threads within a Human Tapestry*, 13.

The Formative Years

Phil Parshall was born November 5, 1937, the youngest of two sons. Phil's father worked for his father in the welding business that the latter had established. Unfortunately, the strained relationship between the two over many years produced negative ripple effects for Phil and others in the family. While Phil's father was never physically violent, his hot temper, complaining spirit, and impulsive behavior resulted in him developing few genuine friendships. Phil's mother was, in fact, the only long-term friend that Phil can recall his father having.[2]

Phil's recollections indicate that the loving relationship Phil's father had with his mother may have been the one positive life pattern that Phil received from him. His parents had an intimate relationship for more than fifty years, most poignantly remembered in Phil's mind by the hours they would sit and talk with each other. He credits their example with helping him to become an incurable romantic with his own wife, Julie. From his mother, Phil learned "discipline, tenacity, and the value of hard work.... . I can only speculate where I would be today without the example and quiet exhortations that consistently flowed from her life."[3]

Phil's other significant early influencers were his grandparents: "My grandfather was always exhorting me to be true to my word ... encouraging me to be a person of integrity." To his "cheerful grandmother," Phil credited the only small religious influence of his childhood. "At some deep level of subconsciousness, I absorbed some of her desire for God."[4]

The Path to Conversion

During Phil's teen years, his father came to have a strong desire to pack up his family and find his fortune in greener pastures. Those pastures included stints in several Florida cities: Palmetto, Tampa/St. Petersburg, and Miami. For part of those years, Phil and his brother, Jimmy, stayed with their grandparents back in Fort Myers, enjoying more stable surroundings and experiencing some of the diversions of misspent youth.

Over the years, and with his grandmother's encouragement, Phil sporadically attended her rather liberal Episcopal church. He was an altar boy for a time and carried the cross in procession. While in Tampa, at another Episcopal church, he also went through what for him was a boring pre-confirmation ordeal of memorizing church creeds. He went on to experience the pomp and ceremony of confirmation conducted by the bishop, but he also

2 Ibid., 14.
3 Ibid., 15–16, 18.
4 Ibid., 18.

knew upon later reflection that he "had no real grasp of any biblical teaching or spiritual reality."[5]

After the brothers rejoined their parents in Miami, following a period with their grandparents, something significant happened in March of 1955 that changed the trajectory of Phil's life. Though he drove alone a considerable distance to attend the early service at an Episcopal church, he said "there was absolutely no cognitive encounter with Christian truth.... But deep in my innermost being was a restless soul waiting to be unleashed."[6]

The catalyst for the next step in the new trajectory in Phil's life came about in a crowded Miami high school hall with a casual invitation from a female student with whom he was acquainted. She invited Phil to attend a cookout that evening "with lots of fellows and gals. Doesn't cost anything. Try and make it. Here's the address."[7]

Phil showed up with another friend, and after a pleasant hour of eating and conversation, he was ready to leave. But just then someone called out for everyone to come inside. The hundred or so teens entered the house and sat on the floor. Phil heard music and testimonies from teens who reverently spoke about Jesus and described their life-changing encounter with him. Then Ray, the owner of the house, spoke for about forty-five minutes, focusing on Ephesians 2:8–9 and emphasizing grace and the free gift of eternal life. When Ray gave an invitation, Phil raised his hand. He prayed with "an extremely pretty girl," who spent more time with him explaining the gospel from John, Romans, and Ephesians: "She asked if I was ready for the Kingdom. With seventy-five percent attention on the message and twenty-five percent attention on the messenger, I said a one hundred percent 'Yes.' A simple prayer followed that revolutionized my life."[8]

Early Discipleship

Over the next six months Phil began the metamorphosis from being "a carnal young man of the world" and a "biblical illiterate" to becoming a responsive and faithful follower of Christ. There were some bumps along the way. One was that Phil fell madly in love with the beautiful young girl who had counseled him to faith. She, however, let him down gently. "She must have realized my ego and spirituality were both at a fragile state." Other ongoing battles were "controlling sexual urges and refraining from cursing."[9]

---

5 Ibid., 27.
6 Ibid.
7 Ibid., 29.
8 Ibid., 29–31.
9 Ibid., 31–32.

A more heartbreaking challenge at this time, though, was trying to help other members of his family find what he found in Christ. After hearing his overly forceful presentation concerning his conversion, his mother told him, "Go to bed and sleep it off. You will have forgotten all about it in the morning." His father, he later learned from his brother, had called the Miami police and asked them to investigate this cult to which their son had become attached. Phil, in reflecting on the frustrating seventeen years before any member of his family became a believer, said, "I attribute much of that delay to my insensitive initial and ongoing presentation of the Gospel."[10]

Ray and Sue became Phil's mentors, and their house became his second home during the months following his conversion. There was a constant flow of young people through the home, and Ray and Sue always had time to counsel and interact with them. Phil commented that "Ray is the most fruitful personal soul winner that I have ever known."[11]

The fellowship and spiritual encouragement Phil received at the "Ranch" (Ray and Sue's home) meant a great deal to him as a graduating senior that spring, particularly since his parents didn't attend his graduation. His father "never felt comfortable in formal situations," and his mother "was probably at work." In spite of this, Phil felt it was an "okay night as I spent it with my new friends from the Ranch."[12]

Personal Growth and Educational Journey

The summer following his high school graduation, Phil took evening summer school classes at the nearby University of Miami while working during the day "grinding and painting metal in an ornamental iron shop." His goal at that point was "to become a wealthy certified public accountant." But during that summer Ray became convinced that Phil "showed potential for the ministry." Even though ministry was not on Phil's list of career options, Ray could be very persuasive. "During one session with him that went well past midnight, I finally gave in and agreed to go ... to Chattanooga to attend Tennessee Temple College, but only for one year."[13]

Phil's arrival at the fundamentalist, independent Baptist Tennessee Temple was quite a culture shock for him and the other fourteen students who arrived from Miami. The sanctions against movies, hand-holding, mixed swimming, etc. were hard to imagine, let alone follow; but eventually the new students got on board and discovered they could survive. Phil majored in Bible, and summarized his time at the school this way:

10 Ibid.
11 Ibid., 32.
12 Ibid., 32–33.
13 Ibid., 33.

Dr. Lee Robertson, the president, was held in highest esteem by all the students. It was my privilege to be baptized by him. Though certainly not an Ivy League school academically, Temple provided a sincere and godly environment which was just perfect for me as a six-month old babe in the Christian faith.[14]

While at Tennessee Temple, Phil heard a great deal about world missions, particularly through the annual missionary conference. The story behind Jim Elliot's martyrdom, accounts of attempts to reach Stone Age natives in Irian Jaya, and descriptions of Islam as "an impregnable barrier to the Gospel" all greatly impacted Phil's emotions. "Gradually the Holy Spirit weaned me from my personal desire for wealth and security, and in 1958 I made my covenant with the Lord for missionary service. I had been a Christian for three years."[15]

As I looked at the lost world statistically, it became evident Islam and Communism were the neglected ideologies that needed Christ. At that time only Muslim countries were open to missionary presence. My heart moved in that direction. A fellow student from Pakistan pressed upon me the need for Christian witness in his country which was 97 percent Muslim. It was not too long before he had a recruit. At last, I had found a cause big enough to live for and, if necessary, to die for.[16]

Prior to his graduation from Tennessee Temple, Phil concluded that he needed further training in missions. Moody Bible Institute was highly recommended to him, and the school's one-year program would meet his needs. So putting aside his budding, but far from cemented, relationship with Julie, he was off to Chicago. While there he learned a lot more about missions, but even more powerful in his life was the Keswick teaching of the possibility of a more victorious experience of spiritual life through seeking a deeper reality of the indwelling Christ. This teaching was well represented among the faculty at Moody, and its message of the "exchanged life," of "not I, but Christ," spoke strongly to Phil.[17]

This hunger for God became almost obsessive. Books were read, Keswick leaders consulted, passionate prayer made, all with the goal of becoming more intimate with my Lord and Savior.... It would, however, take time.... late one afternoon, I entered this empty Prayer Room and began to cry aloud to the Lord for the "higher-plane experience." Oh, how my thirst for God had crescendoed to the point of utter desperation! "Now, Lord, yes, now, send

---

14 Ibid., 34.
15 Ibid., 36–37.
16 Ibid., 37.
17 Ibid., 41–42.

down your refreshing balm for my weary soul. Fill this empty vessel with the reality of your indwelling presence. Lift me to the heavenlies so that I may know release from this debilitating yoke of bondage to sin that so constantly besets me." ...

The next moments defy description and analysis. It was as if the heavens of brass suddenly and inexplicably were cataclysmically torn apart. God was revealed in all his terror and power and love. I stood before him naked and undone. And then it was as if I was tenderly reclothed in new garments ... clean, soft, sweet-smelling, all-embracing garments. I was being enfolded into a mystical oneness with the indwelling Christ.

The next four months were ethereal. Christ was so real, sin so unappealing. Prayer was a delight. Biblical truths ignited within my innermost being. My nervous tension went into remission. How could Christianity possibly get better?[18]

Similar to the period after his conversion, Phil shared rather forcefully with anyone who would listen concerning "the wonders and glories of my experience with the Lord." While this didn't go too badly at Moody, it didn't go particularly well on a brief trip he made back to Tennessee Temple. "I set forth my experience as a norm for all the more 'legalistic' Christians at my alma mater." He encouraged the more phlegmatic Julie, who was still a student at Tennessee Temple, to continue her spiritual journey in exactly the way he had done, and on his return to Chicago he left behind "a confused and bewildered young lady."[19]

The lessons Phil learned through this experience seem to provide some hints to principles that guided his ministry in the years that followed.

Lessons learned: (1) How important it is to have a vital, intimate, ongoing relationship with Christ. (2) God's dealings with his children are tailor made. I have no right to prescribe a formula, but it's okay to make discreet suggestions. (3) Spiritual highs involve the instability of emotions. Without doubt there will be valleys to be endured as well as mountain peaks to be enjoyed. (4) Perseverance throughout the Christian's life is the greatest test of anyone's spiritual experience. I have little patience with this or that prescribed formula which causes the hungry soul to flare upward, and soon leaves nothing but scorched earth. Better steady and lasting than spectacular and temporary.20

---

18 Ibid., 42–43.
19 Ibid., 42.
20 Ibid., 43–44.

Another major influence during Phil's year at Moody was "a revolutionary senior who had for two years been the talk of the Moody campus," a name that is now familiar to many: George Verwer. While Phil initially found zealous George "to be a bit uncouth. He was so compulsive, radical, and denunciatory," he soon discovered another side to him—a side that was humble, gracious, and sensitive. The upshot of this discovery was that Phil spent two and one-half months that summer in Mexico with Operation Mobilization (OM). "In retrospect … I can see my Mexico experience as a microcosm of that which was to come in my missionary career … tension, heat, discouragement, temptation, and failure. Yet character was being formed."[21]

The rest of Phil's educational endeavors included stints at Trinity Evangelical Divinity School and Wheaton Graduate School. These were carried out while he was back from Pakistan/Bangladesh on home assignment with International Christian Fellowship (ICF). Both played significant roles for his academic progress, but most significant for his personal, intellectual, and missiological development was his eventual pursuit of a Doctor of Missiology degree from Fuller Seminary's School of World Mission.

In 1978 Phil and Julie completed a full four and one-half year third term in Bangladesh. "The highlight [of the term] was the beginning of a process that would lead to small Muslim convert fellowships being planted throughout Bangladesh." This was very exciting, but much less encouraging was Phil's growing personal concern about being bogged down in administration. He therefore requested that he and Julie be allowed to go to a totally unevangelized area when they returned from their two-year study leave in the US. His colleagues agreed.[22]

The thought of studying at Fuller Seminary was "like a mirage of water across the distant desert sands. Oh, so desirable, but just not real for me." Nevertheless, Phil decided to enroll in their five extension courses while still in Bangladesh.

> It was a ton of work; listening to the tapes, reading the books and writing 25-page papers for each of the courses. Yet it was exhilarating and extremely relevant to what I was doing. So I decided … [to] seek to enroll in Fuller's residential Doctor of Missiology program. Amazingly, I was accepted, and we began to make plans for a two-year study program.[23]

---

21 Ibid., 47–48.
22 Ibid., 126.
23 Ibid., 125–26.

My entrée at Fuller was helped by my article on Muslim evangelism which came out in a Fall 1978 issue of *Christianity Today*.[24] Perhaps being 41 years old put me in a more senior category as well. The professors, without exception, were totally gracious and helpful. Chuck Kraft even invited me to be his teacher's assistant, an offer I had to refuse because of the academic load I was carrying.[25]

When all was said and done Phil completed graduate studies at Trinity Evangelical Divinity School (MA, summa cum laude), Wheaton Graduate School (MA, magna cum laude), Fuller Theological Seminary (DMiss, summa cum laude), and fellowships at Harvard (1983) and Yale (1993, 2006). He also authored nine books about ministry among Muslims along the way.

Ministry and Writings

It is no stretch to say that Phil Parshall is one of the leading evangelical authorities on ministry to Muslims. He and Julie served as missionaries in Bangladesh from 1962 to 1983, sharing the love of Christ with Muslims there. He served as field director for most of those years. In addition, he was founder of the Bangladesh Bible Correspondence School; founder of an annual spiritual life conference for missionaries in Bangladesh; vice president of the Bangladesh Bible Society; a member of the international council and executive committee of International Christian Fellowship; and interim home director of ICF (1979 to 1980). Following the SIM/ICF merger in 1989, Phil served for almost twenty years as director of the Asian Research Center in the Philippines.

Throughout their ministry years, the Parshalls have represented God's heart for the Muslim world, and Phil has taught extensively, in numerous academic and field locations, regarding Islam and reaching Muslims for Christ.

Concerning the contextualization strategy that is most closely associated with his name, Phil stated this:

> What a great privilege to hammer out a new strategy of evangelism with such a sharp group of enthusiastic, energetic, courageous missionaries. It was entirely a team effort. Unfortunately, the credit (as well as the rather minimal criticism) has flowed in my direction. Never could I have put together such a missiological construct on my own. A few key Muslim converts, as well as each of our missionaries, were the builders. Perhaps my role could best be described as the coordinator. Later, I became the one who unveiled our methodology through my writings. But I want to clearly disassociate myself from any unilateral credit for the efforts and any results that have accrued from the new strategy.[26]

---

24 Parshall, "Evangelizing Muslims: Are There Ways?"
25 Parshall, *Divine Thread*, 127–28.
26 Ibid., 122.

And what was that strategy? Long before the C1-C6 spectrum became a common way to discuss contextualization methods for work among Muslims,[27] Parshall and his missionary expatriates and colleagues were utilizing what would later be characterized as the C4 perspective. This reflected serious contextualization to local and Muslim patterns of life, but with great care not to cross lines into anything that was not biblically permissible. *New Paths in Muslim Evangelism* documents quite thoroughly how they went about it.

Phil's mission's leadership and other missionaries in Bangladesh, both within his mission and outside of it, were supportive of their efforts. Some of the other agencies even commenced their own contextualized outreach among Muslims. Regrettably, many in the already established Bengali churches had a very different reaction initially, but there has been change over time.

> They saw it as a compromise with Islam. The exciting thing is that, over the past 25 years, some within this body of believers have accepted the principles of contextualization and launched out to establish a number of quasi-homogeneous Muslim convert churches.[28]

Among Parshall's most popular writings are the following books:

- *The Fortress and the Fire, Gospel Literature Service*, Bombay, 1974 (with Spanish and Chinese editions).

- *New Paths in Muslim Evangelism*, Baker, 1980. Reprinted by Authentic Publishing in 2003 as *Muslim Evangelism* (with Chinese, Korean, and Romanian editions).

- *Bridges to Islam*, Baker, 1983. Reprinted by Authentic Publishing in 2007 (with Indonesian edition).

- *Beyond the Mosque*, Baker, 1985.

- *The Cross and the Crescent*, Tyndale, 1989 (with French and Korean editions). Reprinted by Gabriel Publishing in 2002.

- *Inside the Community*, Baker, 1994. Reprinted by Baker in 2002 as *Understanding Muslim Teachings and Traditions*.

- *The Last Great Frontier*, Open Doors, 2000.

- *Divine Threads within A Human Tapestry* (Memoirs), William Carey Library, 2000 (with Korean edition).

- *Lifting the Veil: The World of Muslim Women*, Gabriel Publishing, 2003 (with German edition).

(Four of these books are now published by InterVarsity.)

---

27 Travis, "The C1 to C6 Spectrum."
28 Parshall, *Divine Thread*, 122–23.

Phil has also written a number of more general missions-related articles. Seldom inclined to keep his strongly held views hidden under a bushel, several of his articles may have inspired even more exuberant dialogue than his groundbreaking early writings on contextualized Muslim ministry. Just a couple of examples will follow.

The July 1990 issue of *EMQ* includes an article Phil wrote about missionary productivity, and more particularly on factors hindering a higher caliber of it.[29] He cited poor accountability stemming from an independence mentality and inadequate administrative structures in many agencies, as well as electronic diversions and recreational escapism due to discouragement. He did point out that these things tend not to be a problem for highly motivated and innovative missionaries, but that the problem is widespread among disorganized and laid-back workers. Not many were talking about the problem at the time. In his memoir, Phil also cites a fixation on avoiding failure of any kind. He considered this a powerful hindrance to "careful, calculated, risk-taking," a characteristic of the apostle Paul that he tried to emulate.[30]

His "most controversial missiological proposal," however, and one that has had a very long lifespan of feedback, is another *EMQ* article Phil wrote, entitled "A Small Family Is a Happy Family."[31] The title was originally a Bangladeshi slogan for promoting birth control.

> I simply made a pragmatic case for missionaries to limit their families to two children. Issues like support, logistics, schooling, illness potential etc. were mentioned, with a conclusion that I have observed few large families remain on the mission field for an extended period... .
>
> Overall, I stand by my thesis and await statistical proof to convince me otherwise. Incidentally, just to make sure I do not become overly dogmatic, the Lord arranged for our daughter to marry an MK who has four siblings and whose parents ministered in the Philippines in excess of 30 years![32]

January 10, 1984, marked the beginning of a new chapter in the Parshalls' ministry. Following on the heels of an earlier survey trip (in 1981) and negotiations between several mission groups, Phil and Julie arrived in Manila with a new vision and task. Recognizing that the southern island of Mindanao and its one million Muslims was the least evangelized part of the Philippines, three agencies—SEND International, Overseas Missionary Fellowship (OMF), and Phil's agency, International Christian Fellowship (ICF, soon to become part of SIM)—had committed together to an outreach to the Muslims of

---

29 Parshall, "Why Some People Are Unproductive."
30 Parshall, *Divine Thread*, 187.
31 Parshall, "A Small Family Is a Happy Family."
32 Parshall, *Divine Thread*, 186.

Mindanao. The Parshalls would reside in Manila, engaged in what appeared to be the first direct outreach to Muslims in that great city, and Phil would also serve as consultant to the emerging team that the consortium was fielding in Mindanao.[33]

> To be brutally honest, my vision was intermixed with an unhealthy measure of pride. I had been part of a team that had seen a major evangelistic breakthrough in Bangladesh. I felt it would be relatively easy to guide this flexible, young team into a methodological approach that had already proven itself in one Asian setting. At our quarterly strategy sessions, I was quick to cross-reference every problem with a ready-made solution which had been successful in Bangladesh. Great credit must be given to the Consortium team for their patience and grace in putting up with me during those years.

> The struggles and results of the next nine years of Consortium life are documented in chapter 15 [of this same book, Phil's memoir *Divine Threads*]. None of us ever expected that the battle would be so devastatingly intense. Perhaps there are lessons to be learned from our failures that can be helpful to other teams just entering into the fray of Muslim evangelism.[34]

The daily grind in the reading room on a dirty and pollution-filled street in the Muslim quarter of Manila was no picnic, either. While verbal abuse and rejection of his message was the usual outcome, Phil continued his efforts, he said, because he never wanted to become an armchair strategist, and because most Muslims in Manila had never even heard a presentation of the gospel.[35]

By far the most difficult experience, however, during the Parshalls' years in the Philippines came in June of 1991. "Never has the death of anyone so affected me as has the despicable murder of 33-year-old John Speers. I had bonded so very deeply with John and his lovely family for the 18 months prior to his being killed." Shortly after the event had happened, Phil recorded the following:

> "John Speers has just been shot in the back of the head and is dead." These incredible words came to me on the phone in our Detroit apartment just three hours after John was murdered by a Muslim who was probably high on drugs. Within two hectic hours, I was on the expressway heading toward the airport to fly back to Manila. John had been with his family in Mindanao for a concentrated month of language study when this senseless tragedy occurred. It seemed simply to have been a 'thrill killing' without political or religious motivation.

---

33 Ibid., 157–58.
34 Ibid., 158.
35 Ibid., 159–60.

For ten days, I sought to minister comfort to Brenda and to her family who flew out, and to their innumerable friends.[36]

An infinitely more encouraging note to end our discussion of the Parshalls' ministry in the Philippines is what the Lord chose to do among many of the churches in the Philippines. A new heart and mobilization for outreach to Muslims in their land has grown exponentially in recent years, in no small part due to the involvement of Phil and Julie and others with them. Given the almost four-hundred-year animosity between Christians and Muslims in the nation, this has had an impact both there and in many other parts of the globe.[37]

Phil's Legacy

Others in this collection of articles honoring Phil Parshall will be writing in some depth concerning ideological and methodological connections that exist between him and others, some of whom preceded him and many of whom built upon his work and insights. It is both unnecessary and beyond the scope of this piece to attempt the same.

As an alternative, I shall endeavor to list in brief the contributions, some well-known and many unheralded, that can legitimately be credited to the life and work of Phil Parshall.

1. His name is synonymous with more contextualized, and incredibly more effective, evangelistic approaches in reaching Muslims with the gospel of Jesus Christ. The methods that he and others pioneered bore much fruit in the 1970s in Bangladesh; and his publication of *New Paths in Muslim Evangelization* marked the beginning of an epoch-initiating change in approach that has seen more Muslims finding salvation in Jesus Christ in the last forty-five years than occurred in all the prior fourteen centuries put together.

2. His multiple books on Islam and Muslim evangelization are widely considered to be essential reading today for anyone considering outreach among the world's 1.3 billion Muslims.

3. His ubiquitous teaching on Islam and Muslim outreach through Perspectives courses and at numerous colleges and seminaries has been instrumental in many choosing to follow Christ into missional engagement with Muslim peoples. His field seminars have encouraged and assisted many others.

---

36 Ibid., 195.
37 Information gleaned through personal interaction with the Parshalls and other missionaries and church leaders from the Philippines.

4. He is one to speak the truth as he understands it, yet he is humble enough to do so in love, recognizing the Lord's command to do so, and that the Lord alone is the ultimate arbiter of where truth and motivations lie. His October 1998 *EMQ* article, "Danger! New Directions in Contextualization," may be the clearest example of the former; and the 2004 *EMQ* piece, "Lifting the Fatwa," may be the clearest example of the latter. In the latter, he wants to make very clear that he honors and respects the sincerity and work of those who see biblical contextualization truth differently than he does.

5. He is a team player and selfless enough to serve at different times in leadership (which he never particularly liked), as field leader in Bangladesh for many years and for a brief period as the US director for ICF.

6. He is a big-picture thinker who understands the recruitment, oversight, and financial challenges faced by a relatively small mission like ICF, and he was instrumental in bringing about the merger with SIM in 1989. I had arranged an itinerary and accompanied Phil on a workshop tour in West Africa a few years earlier, and that in turn led to the first of several SIMCOME (SIM Consultation on Muslim Evangelism) gatherings of SIM workers. Phil was invited as a resource person. Unlike some of the instances already described from his youth, he had certainly learned the balance described in point 4 above by this time, and his interaction with SIM leaders at that event was a key step leading to merger.

7. His work in the Philippines was a key factor in initiating a movement of church mobilization for outreach to Muslims. This is amazing considering the great animosity that existed between the Christian and Muslim communities for several hundred years in that land.

There are, no doubt, many other things that could be mentioned here about Phil Parshall; but I will close with this: Phil is the kind of friend we should all wish to be. He is like a bulldog in keeping relationships strong. He cares deeply for people, and he has found joy in his retirement years, being a servant to many.

References

Parshall, P. 1977. "A Small Family Is a Happy Family." *Evangelical Missions Quarterly* 13 (4): 210.

———. 1979. "Evangelizing Muslims: Are There Ways?" *Christianity Today* 23 (7): 28.

———. 1990. "Why Some People Are Unproductive." *Evangelical Missions Quarterly* 26 (3): 251–53.

———. 1998. "Danger! New Directions in Contextualization." *Evangelical Missions Quarterly* 34 (4): 404–6, 409–10.

———. 2000. *Divine Threads within a Human Tapestry: Memoirs of Phil Parshall.* Pasadena, CA: William Carey Library.

———. 2004. "Lifting the Fatwa." *Evangelical Missions Quarterly* 40 (3): 288–93.

Travis, J. 1998. "The C1 to C6 Spectrum: A Practical Tool for Defining Six Types of 'Christ-centered Communities' ('C') Found in the Muslim Context." *Evangelical Missions Quarterly* 34 (4): 411–15.

2 STANDING ON THE SHOULDERS OF OTHERS
Kevin Higgins

When Innovations Surprise the Innovator

Among other things, I am a quasi-closet musician, or singer-songwriter. One genre I have studied and learned from is the broad category known as folk music, and the best definition I have heard of folk music is that of Marcus Mumford (of Mumford and Sons), which was basically like this: Folk means people, so folk music belongs to people.

Implied in that remark is the insight that succeeding generations of artists and songwriters stand on the shoulders and learn from and even incorporate the music and lyrics of prior generations. This is actually true of all music, but folk music admits this fact, and celebrates it.

In the same way, whether we speak of music or mission:

Every innovation stands on the shoulders of prior innovations.
Every innovator stands on the shoulders of prior innovators.

That is true of me in my music, and it is true for me in my life in mission. And one of the innovators (there are many) upon whose shoulders I stand is Phil Parshall.

My History with Phil Parshall

Phil and I only met in person one time, and over the years I am aware that some of what I have written about and practiced and advocated for has gone beyond the limits with which he has felt were warranted biblically and missiologically.

But let me describe my journey.

I first "met" Phil in the early 1980s. I was newly married, and by divine accident I had become involved working with Iranians in the Los Angeles area. I was grasping for anything I could find to help, and found two giants.

The first was Don McCurry, at the Zwemer Institute. I attended the seminars, met with Don, and learned all I could.

The second was Phil's book (perhaps his best-known work), *New Paths in Muslim Evangelism*. I remember reading it. I remember being impressed by it. But frankly, I had no experiential grid yet through which to absorb or appropriate the insights he shared. He was one voice in my journey toward a sense of call to work with Muslims.

A few years later, midway through my seminary studies, my wife and I were invited to teach at a Bible school in Uganda. We agreed, seeing the position as a way to test a calling to mission by going to a different culture, albeit one that did not particularly need missionaries. This exposure to missions was a way to test the cross-cultural part of our call before testing the Muslim part.

Unfortunately, the Bible school never opened that year; nevertheless we found ourselves engaged in building relationships with Somalis in the little town in Uganda where we were living. God indeed used our experiences that year to confirm the two parts of what we sensed was our calling (i.e., working cross-culturally, and working with Muslims). It was also a year that brought us face-to-face with some of the barriers to fulfilling that calling.

Let me be transparent and say that some of those barriers were within us. This realization led to a journey of deeper growth in our own souls—healing our pasts and addressing our own unhealthy pieces as people (especially mine!). But that year in Uganda, working in a relational way among Somalis (almost by accident), drove me back again to a similar place I had found myself in while working with Iranians in Los Angeles: I was in need of help and mentors. I found three.

In the process, I purchased my first Qur'an, and the first of my mentors that I will mention here was actually the Imam who began to teach me Qur'anic Arabic.

The second was an author I discovered by accident in a Nairobi bookstore: Giulio Basetti-Sani, who wrote *The Koran in the Light of Christ*.[1]

I am not suggesting Phil would enjoy being included with these two, but he was the third of my mentors. I returned to his book, *New Paths*, and found my life experience had caught up with the book. I found it speaking to me and helpful to me in so many practical ways. I will come back to this later.

It was some time before Phil and I crossed paths again, and the next meeting was face-to-face. I returned from Uganda, finished seminary, and then worked for several years in an urban church context (including an attempt at church planting among out-patient mental health patients). Interestingly, at least to me, the insights in *New Paths*, which were originally focused on adapting discipleship practices to fit Muslim contexts, also had a profound impact on how I understood the work of church planting in an urban US context.

---

1 Giulio Basetti-Sani, *The Koran in the Light of Christ*. Chicago: Franciscan Herald Press, 1977.

Around that time, our first children were born, we bought a house, and were settling in. But God intervened and the call to cross-cultural life among Muslims was rekindled. In 1990 we began to prepare to move to South Asia. I took up reading *New Paths* again while we did support raising, and then arrived in South Asia in 1991, ready to put the book into practice. Or so I thought.

I ended up serving with a national church that deeply opposed such attempts at contextual approaches and took a very strong view of the—dare I say—evil origins of the Islamic religion. For a year I tried to integrate my past learning with the insights of my new colleagues. I learned their language and culture and worked hard at our various responsibilities (including running a business).

Eventually we ran into visa problems and needed to leave, returning to the US just in time to hear two men speak at my seminary about work going on elsewhere in South Asia. They spoke of a large movement, and I remember thinking to myself, "If this is even 10 percent true, I need to learn from these people." I spoke to them—one being an American and the other the leader of the movement. I was invited to join them and help them with the business they were developing. My aim, while being willing to help, was to learn and return to the country in which we had originally been called to serve.

And learn I did.

This was still the early and middle 1990s, when things like the "C Scale" were just beginning to be talked about.[2] The term "insider movement" had not yet been coined.[3] In fact, any talk of "movements" at all was at best in only the very earliest of beginnings. But I was experiencing and seeing one up close and in person.

The movement had attracted attention, of course, and a decision was made to include it in what was intended to be a three-foci study including this South Asian movement and two other contexts in sub-Saharan Africa. I had the privilege of being a part of the team that designed, conducted, and wrote up the field research in South Asia. And it is this study which led to my actual meeting with Phil.

While the research was still going on, I believe, I was introduced to Phil. We met, as I recall, at Phil's home. I knew that that these brothers were not in full agreement on any number of things. Phil was gracious and generous with his time and conversation.

---

2 There have been numerous articles and discussions of the C Scale. I give one example in the references.
3 For discussions about insider movements from different perspectives, see the Lausanne discussion, for example, at https://www.lausanne.org/lgc-transfer/highly-contextualized-missions-surveying-the-global-conversation.

Some months later, perhaps as much as two years, Phil was given a copy of the results once we had completed the research. That led to my next "meeting," not in person, but in the form of an article Phil wrote for *EMQ*.[4] Since the article included the word *danger* in the title, the reader can correctly surmise that Phil was not an enthusiastic supporter of what was happening in the movement.

I know from Phil's later writing that he knows what it is like for a scholar to have godly colleagues wonder about the implications of his own work. He was also challenged by those who felt he had gone too far, or that his ideas would lead others to do so. He describes this in his memoir.[5]

And it is this reality that brings me to the main point of relating the history of my connection with Phil, largely though his ideas and thinking: Phil was an innovator. He faced the challenges all innovators face. He needed the courage all innovators need. And his courage in the face of such critique should be applauded by those who follow and build on his innovative work. I count myself as one who applauds.

At the same time, innovators do enable later innovators to begin from a different vantage point than was available as they themselves sought to probe new territory. I self-consciously stand on the shoulders of men and women like Phil Parshall; and to return to my metaphor of folk music, I feel I have recombined his melodies and lyrics in new ways. I am grateful.

Lessons I Have Learned

I have hinted already at some of what I have learned. I want to touch on two main areas. The first is missiological, and the second is personal. And I will limit myself to two examples of each.

I want to outline the missiological "gleanings" I have attained from several books Phil has written and I have studied, and suggest ways I have been enabled by them to continue to press in, or seek beyond (not to suggest Phil would agree with every new insight or experiment that I feel he enabled me to imagine, of course).

Distinguish between Form and Function

First, Phil's application of what he learned at Fuller School of World Mission encouraged me on my own path of integrating the social sciences and the Scriptures to examine and critique mission practice. It was liberating to be introduced to his practice of probing the consequences of contextualizing so-called Christian "forms" (which were often Western) in order to allow truly biblical "functions" to flourish in a cross-cultural setting. An older mentor, even

4 Parshall, "Danger! New Directions in Contextualization."
5 Parshall, *Divine Threads within a Human Tapestry.*

at a distance through his written works, can grant validation to the younger traveler who gains a sense of confidence from those who have gone before. That was true for me.

I have in some ways taken that contextualization process further than Phil originally imagined, or in ways that would subsequently make him feel a certain unease. So I want to be careful in what I say, lest it appear that I am assuming Phil would equally celebrate everything I envision as the natural implications of his seed-work. But I do feel as if I have stood on the shoulders of a prior explorer and benefited from his map-making as I (in my understanding) have been able to journey further in the trajectory of the path on which his ideas set me going.

Listen to Others

Second, Phil's books modeled an attempt to listen well to what Muslims themselves thought and felt. In saying this, I refer to his relationships with Muslim friends, as well as his reading of Muslim texts. This too encouraged me on my journey on the path toward realizing the importance of more than the Qur'an in that process.

Eventually, as one example of his influence in my life, this led to my studies in how Muslims approached the translation/interpretation of the Qur'an. I tried to listen well, and in so doing I found insights and wisdom which can inform Christians about the task of translation of the Bible.[6] Phil was one of the early sources of such inspiration.

Practice Humility in Relationships

In the arena of what I have learned from Phil in terms of relationships, I want to also mention two examples. Both, actually, spring from a certain kind of manner which is evident in his written work.

The first is the humility with which Phil describes his own struggles with seeking to live a godly life. He is very honest in his memoirs about the struggles that missionaries face in a number of areas (e.g., marriage, sexual temptations, and more). But he does not point the finger. He is vulnerable enough to include himself. Such transparency is as freeing to younger leaders in the realm of spiritual growth as is his pioneering of experimentation in missiology.

I have sought to lead, as well, from a place of humble transparency. I have learned about the value of humility by observing a number of people in my life over the years. Phil's voice is among them.

---

6 For example, the way that Muslims incorporate the original text of the Qur'an and in some cases include both a very literal translation and in the same publication a more explanatory translation.

The second is Phil's willingness to show how his own spiritual life falls short in comparison to some of his Muslim friends. This exhibits the same humility I just cited. He mentions this in *New Paths*[7] and also in his memoirs,[8] thus at the earlier and later stages of his written work. This consistent posture suggests to me that humility was part of the fabric of Phil's inner life.

In recent years, just as the term "insider" has emerged as a way of speaking of believers and movements, so too has the term "alongsider" emerged as an increasingly common way to speak of missionaries. The term has been coined to try to find vocabulary that captures the humble, servant, learning posture many of us are seeking to embrace. And many of us have learned the hard way how to be alongsiders—finding our pride and presumption broken by experience. We become alongsiders through our willingness to learn from others (from insiders, from other missionaries, and from Muslims who do not yet believe). While Phil never used the word *alongsider*, he modeled some early elements. And once again I reckon my journey is in part, at least, a result of standing on the shoulders of things he spoke and wrote.

Phil also would not have used the term "holy envy," by which some have tried to express a posture of intentionally looking for the best in other religions—in their religious practices and their religious followers. This attitude is not employed to diminish the so-called dark sides of religions. But it is a posture that assumes a charitable assumption about others, while also being willing to look honestly at the dark sides of our own religious traditions.

Again, I see seeds of this in Phil's own life and work. I know he would not welcome all the comparisons or align himself with all that some people mean when they speak of holy envy. This is yet another area where I see myself and others, in our own various perspectives, standing upon the shoulders of those like Phil, able to discover things we could not have seen or obtained otherwise.

Concluding Thoughts

I want to return to some of my opening remarks about folk music. In 1965, at the Newport Folk Festival, Pete Seeger (a patriarch of the folk music movement) reportedly tried to cut the cables that powered the amplifiers Bob Dylan was using to take electrify his sound. Dylan played his old music; he just re-presented it in a new sound (and louder, of course).

This response reminds me of how the Athenians resisted Paul on Mars Hill (Acts 17:22–34). At that rock festival, some in the audience, including Peter Seeger, hated the music; some loved it; some reserved judgment. Dylan took a risk. He innovated, but it was not a risk he would have ever been in a position

7 Parshall, *New Paths in Muslim Evangelism.*
8 Parshall, *Divine Threads within a Human Tapestry.*

to make had people like Seeger not pioneered the folk music movement to begin with.

By taking the risk of documenting his thinking and ideas in written forms, as well as by his own living of his life, Phil Parshall has added to the canon, as it were, of the folk music of missiology and mission practice. Others like me stand on his shoulders, and we have taken some aspects of his portfolio to places Phil would not be comfortable going. However, a generation of missiologists are very aware that they would not be standing where they are if not for the innovative spirit of Phil Parshall.

References

Basetti-Sani, G. 1977. *The Koran in the Light of Christ.* Chicago: Franciscan Herald Press.

Parshall, P. 1980. *New Paths in Muslim Evangelism.* Grand Rapids: Baker.

———. 1998. "Danger! New Directions in Contextualization." *Evangelical Missions Quarterly* 34 (4): 404–6, 409–10.

———. 2000. *Divine Threads within a Human Tapestry: Memoirs of Phil Parshall.* Pasadena, CA: William Carey Library.

3

ONLY ONE OFFENSE[1]
Miriam Adeney

Why Cultural Immersion Still Matters

My father and mother were born in the most beautiful place on earth, in the foothills of the Appalachians... . It was a place where gray mists hid the tops of low, deep-green mountains, where red-bone and bluetick hounds flashed through the pines as they chased possums into the sacks of old men in frayed overalls, where old women in bonnets ... shelled purple hulls, canned peaches, and made biscuits too good for this world. It was a place where the first frost meant hog killin' time and the mouthwatering smell of cracklins would drift for acres from the giant bubbling pots. It was a place where the screams of panthers, like a woman's anguished cry, still haunted remote ridges and hollows in the dead of night.[2]

That is how author Rick Bragg remembered pork in his Appalachian upbringing.

Think about pork. Ribs dripping barbeque sauce slurped with friends at backyard suppers. Pork roast, mashed potatoes, green beans, and apple pie at special Sunday dinners when all the relatives come to visit. Hot dogs at baseball games, with bats slamming and balls soaring. Pork tacos. Pork tamales. Sausages and pancakes on lazy winter weekends.

All those memories and aromas. Would you give them up? Phil Parshall did. He quit eating pork because culture matters. And culture is not just ideas and words and kinship charts. Culture is material. It is gritty. You can taste culture. In fact, the cuisine is one of the first identifiable elements of a culture.

---

1 Material in this chapter draws from several of the author's publications, including *Kingdom Without Borders: The Untold Story of Global Christianity* (InterVarsity, 2009); "Telling Stories: Contextualization and American Missiology," in *Global Missiology for the 21ˢᵗ Century*, ed. William Taylor (Baker Academic, 2000); "Is God Colorblind or Colorful? Gospel, Globalization and Ethnicity," in *One World or Many?* ed. Richard Tiplady (William Carey Library, 2003); "The Myth of the Blank Slate: A Check List for Short-Term Missions," in *Effective Engagement in Short-Term Missions*, ed. Robert Priest (William Carey Library, 2008); "Colorful Initiatives: North American Diasporas in Mission," *Missiology* 39, no. 1 (January 2011); and "Why Cultures Matter," *International Journal of Frontier Missiology* 32, no. 2 (Summer 2015).
2 Bragg, *All Over But the Shoutin'*, 3.

Muslims repudiate pork. In China, where the Muslim Hui people merge into the majority Han in many ways, abstinence from pork draws a distinguishing line. Among the Cambodian Muslim Cham, during the genocidal years under the Khmer Rouge, people died because of pork. When pork was served at communal meals, those Cambodians who did not eat it were identified as stubborn, god-fearing Muslims rather than atheistic Marxists, and they were executed. Pork matters.

So Parshall turned away from the hot dogs and the pork roasts and the ribs, and instead learned to eat goat.

But was Parshall's abstinence necessary? Yes, perhaps it was important during the 70s, 80s, and 90s. Today, however, cultural differences may be eroding. Distinctives seems to be flattening out. The whole world drinks Coca Cola, watches *Star Wars*, orders over the internet—and the whole world, as of this writing, is being devastated by a coronavirus. Wherever they are found around the globe, government officials and business leaders and academicians and scientists share similar issues, hopes, and fears. Students take similar exams. Doctors and nurses follow similar protocols. Pilots adhere to common guidelines. Languages can be translated by artificial intelligence (A-I) devices, polished by native speakers. Overall, lifeways are becoming more homogenous. In our era, there are a lot of Muslims who are comfortable in Western countries. Some even eat pork.

Of course, there are exceptions. Poorer citizens may not have easy access to the internet. They may lack literacy altogether. And global media can stoke ethnic passions. South Sudanese or Tibetans, for example, can find each other worldwide and raise a common voice more powerfully than ever before.

Nevertheless, it is clear that cultures are not pristine separate entities. Over time, cultures change. And at any given moment they display variation. A third-generation Arab in Europe may not speak or read Arabic and may scoff at Arab traditional values. How important is culture for him? Even in the home countries, cultures may be diluted by globalization, as West African novelist Sembene Ousmane laments:

> Take myself, father of a family, and others like me. We are no longer typical, living examples for our children. It's the cinema, the TV, the video which are the channels for the new cultures, the new values. We, the older generation, are absent in our own families.

> I was born in the colonial era. I witnessed all the humiliation and self-abasement my father had to put up with in order to survive. But in the evenings when we came home to our huts, we rediscovered our culture. It was a refuge. We were ourselves again, we were free. Nowadays the TV is right

there inside the hut where in the old days the father, the mother, the aunt held sway and the grandma told her stories and legends. Even that time is now taken away from us. So we are left with a society which is growing more and more impoverished, emptying itself of its creative substance, turning more and more to values it does not create.[3]

How important are cultures today? This question has implications for mission strategy. How much time and attention should missionaries devote to studying cultures? Billions of people have not yet heard clearly that Jesus is Lord. Millions lack clean water, and prenatal and postnatal care, and schooling, and jobs that can support a family. As Americans who are pragmatically oriented, resourced, and skilled, we can tackle those kinds of issues. We know how to plan and get results. Our donors expect that. Shouldn't we move forward efficiently? Why get bogged down in a study of culture which may be obsolete?

With particular attention to Phil Parshall's seminal, groundbreaking book, *New Paths in Muslim Evangelism,* this chapter explores those questions. Missiology has developed considerably since that work was published. Parshall himself has put forward other ideas and moved in slightly different directions. Yet several false views on culture still plague mission work. These include

- Essentialism: Cultures have unchangeable cores and characteristics.

- Globalism: Cultural differences are disappearing due to global media, travel, and business.

- Entitlement: Minority cultures' oppression is the most essential interpretive framework.

- Pragmatism: Cultures are tools that we use in order to communicate effectively and accomplish our goals.

While there is a kernel of truth in each of these emphases, if they are left unchecked they can skew and warp our ministry. This chapter will touch on some of the dangers. Parshall believed a missionary should take culture seriously enough to adapt until "only the core message—the gospel—would offend."[4] In this he followed the apostle Paul (1 Cor 1, 8, 9, 10, 14). Inevitably, the cross of Jesus is a scandal and a stumbling block. It offends our pride. It upsets our self-contained worlds. Although the offense of the cross may be inescapable, all other offenses should be avoided, Parshall urged. Let no cultural gaffes impede the clear and loving communication of the world-shattering gospel.

To honor local cultures, Parshall was willing to venture, willing to try, willing to move through uncharted seas. Because he dared, we all are richer. How does this apply today? That is the question this chapter will explore.

---

3 Gadjigo, *Ousmane Sembene,* 244.
4 Parshall, *New Paths in Muslim Evangelism,* 61.

God and Cultures: "The Cross-Cultural Communicator"

In a chapter of *New Paths* entitled "The Cross-Cultural Communicator," Parshall reflected on culture areas like money, housing, time, dress, food, family interactions, and language. Overall, he favored immersion in and adaptation to the culture. Parshall pointed to Jesus as his model. The incarnate Jesus was not "global." Jesus never ate pizza or cheeseburgers—just fish and hummus. Jesus never spoke English or French. He could have zapped communication to all the diverse language speakers on earth through a comprehensive cosmic code. But he did not. Instead, he spoke Aramaic and Greek and Hebrew. He *limited* himself. Philippians 2 uses this verb to refer to Jesus' becoming a human being. Beyond that unimaginable limitation, Jesus went further, and limited himself to living as a Palestinian Jew—a relatively poor carpenter in a society oppressed by a colonial power.

"Why didn't Jesus come as a Chinese person? The most advanced civilizations at that time were in China and South America," asked one of my Chinese friends. He concluded, "Becoming a Palestinian Jew simply shows God's sovereignty and grace." Why didn't Jesus come as a Chinese person, or a German, or a Spaniard? Jesus honored the particularity of place that God had begun centuries earlier when he selected Abraham to be a channel of his revelation to all peoples (Gen 12:3). Abraham's descendants were called to share God's story globally. They failed badly. Yet God's successive revelations to and through them laid a foundation for Jesus' full message.

At the same time, while Jesus modeled a love for the local, he also affirmed foreigners. Although he was a dyed-in-the-wool Jew, he did not expect foreigners to change their ethnic identity or their culture. He met them and honored them as they were (Matt 25:33; Mark 7:26; Luke 7:2; John 4).

The Incarnation was not the beginning of God's involvement with cultures, however. What is the origin of cultures? In the beginning, God created people in his image. He endowed people with a smidgeon of creativity. Expressing this creativity, people everywhere imagined and developed cultural patterns—cuisines, housing styles, family arrangements, agriculture techniques, economic exchanges, community groupings, governments, conflict-resolution strategies, games, music, and philosophies. These diverse patterns are the result of God's gift of creativity. As one poet said,

> When God made the world, he could have finished it. But he didn't. He left it as a raw material—to tease us, to tantalize us, to set us thinking, and experimenting, and risking, and adventuring. And therein we find our supreme interest in living.

He gave us the challenge of raw materials, not the satisfaction of perfect, finished things.

He left the music unsung, and the dramas unplayed.

He left the poetry undreamed, in order that men and women might not become bored, but engaged in stimulating, exciting, creative activities that keep them thinking, working, experimenting, and experiencing all the joys and satisfactions of achievement.[5]

God created us in his image, gifted us with creativity, and set us in a world of possibilities and challenges. Applying our gift, we have developed the cultures of the world. In the beginning, God affirmed that it was not good for humans to be alone. So he gave his blessing to cultural areas such as the family, the state, work, worship, arts, education, and even festivals. He gave attention to laws which preserved a balanced ecology, ordered social relations, provided for sanitation, and protected the rights of the weak, the blind, the deaf, widows, orphans, foreigners, the poor, and debtors.

He affirmed the physical world out of which material culture is developed. He delighted in the very soil and rivers that he gave his people. It was "a land the LORD your God cares for" (Deut 11:12 NIV). God recognizes and affirms the material pleasures of his people he placed them in.

For the LORD your God is bringing you into a good land—a land with brooks, streams, and deep springs gushing out into the valleys and hills; a land with wheat and barley, vines and fig trees, pomegranates, olive oil and honey; a land where bread will not be scarce and you will lack nothing; a land where the rocks are iron and you can dig copper out of the hills. (Deut 8:7–9 NIV)

In the picture language of the Old Testament, God gave people oil to make their faces shine, wine to make their hearts glad, friends to sharpen them like iron, wives like fruitful vines, and children like arrows shot out of their bows. The result is culture. Economic, social, and artistic patterns combine to make up a culture, and the potential to develop these is a gift of God.

Cultures are treasure chests of symbols for exuberant expression of the image of God.

Considered globally, the rich mix of cultures enriches God's world. Like a mosaic, like a kaleidoscope, this diversity appears in biblical texts about God's kingdom at the end of time from Isaiah chapter 60 to Revelation chapters 7, 20, and 21. Here we see representatives from all peoples and tribes and languages, in all their particularity and distinctness, worshiping around God's throne. The God who creates billions of unique snowflakes and personalities, who

5 Stockdale, "God Left the Challenge in the Earth," 20.

dazzles with diverse colors, who infuses our air with aromas, who spangles a boggling array of fish across the oceans, who layers the earth under the soil with diverse granites from grey to red to white to black—this God delights in diversity. He is the one who has generated the possibility for cultures in all their variations.

This is one-sided, however. A huge part of human life is missing from the previous paragraphs. Customs that glorify God are not the only reality that we observe around us. Instead, institutions that promote justice are twisted. Cultural patterns that promote holiness are often sadly lacking. Exploitation and idolatry pulse through our societies. How well we know the corruption, the waste, the lust, the power grabbing, the environmental degradation, the marginalization of vulnerable populations. Every culture reeks of selfishness. People everywhere wound each other again and again.

We are not only created in God's image; we are also sinners. That is the tragic truth. Our cultures reflect the sin as well as the image. We are called, then, not only to appreciate our culture but also to confront it—to affirm God's good gifts, and simultaneously to judge the patterns of idolatry and exploitation.

The New Testament's contrasting descriptions of "the powers" are relevant here. On one hand, the powers that give order to our lives—government, education, media, religion, sports, art, family—are gifts of God: "In [Christ] all things were created: things in heaven and on earth, visible and invisible, whether thrones or powers or rulers or authorities; all things have been created through him and for him. He is before all things, and in him all things hold together" (Col 1:16–17 NIV). On the other hand, we humans often turn these good gifts into idols. We give some of the powers too much importance. Before long we are using them exploitatively. Then it is time to confront the powers, to "wrestle" against them (Eph 6:12). Of course, the greatest confrontation was Jesus' death and resurrection, whereby he defeated the powers and ushered in a new kind of power: "Having disarmed the powers and authorities, he made a public spectacle of them, triumphing over them by the cross" (Col 2:15 NIV). The "powers" in these verses refer both to spiritual entities and to cultural institutions that have become de facto idols.

Who confronts the evils in a culture? Indigenous leaders who are immersed in the Word and the Spirit should be at the forefront. Even poorly educated leaders may be guided by the Spirit quite remarkably if they seriously want to follow what little of the Word they may have. Such leaders should not be lone rangers, but should practice fellowship and community, with mutual humility and accountability.

When considering what needs to be confronted, Parshall's book *New Paths* warns against syncretism. Syncretism involves adaptation so substantial that the resulting behavior is inconsistent with the gospel. Where and when and how much should believers from Muslim background adapt to their culture? Where should they draw a line? Missiologists continue to struggle with this. A useful model may be provided by Dean Gilleland's article "How 'Christian' Are African Independent Churches?" Gilleland asked this question because some African-originated churches, involving millions of people, seemed to practice paganism. Charms, magical formulas, and fortunetelling were more familiar to their members than the rich story of Jesus. Some leaders even presented themselves as divine. In this context, Gilleland suggested five points for evaluation,[6] which I have summarized here:

1. How central is Jesus? Do members use his name merely as a magical mantra, or do they listen to his teachings and obey them? Do they understand what his death and resurrection mean?

2. How central is the Bible? Are members studying it, committing its teachings to their hearts and expressing them in action? Or do they consider the Bible merely an object with esoteric power?

3. How central are baptism and the Lord's supper, two sacraments that Jesus commended?

4. Are heretics disciplined? Or are deviations allowed to flourish unchecked?

5. What direction is the movement heading? Is it becoming more Christ-centered and more biblical? Or less so?

As we try to honor local cultures, such guidelines may help us avoid syncretism. God ordained cultural diversity. Jesus affirmed local culture. We want to rejoice in God's good gifts, yet confront evil patterns, following indigenous leaders who are immersed in the Word and the Spirit. In the opening section of this chapter, I listed several false views about culture. The theology of culture I have outlined here applies to two of them: Entitlement and Pragmatism. Entitlement—a minority culture's insistence that oppression is the key framework for understanding culture—confronts culture too much. It does not sufficiently appreciate the positive aspects of every culture. Pragmatism—viewing cultures merely as tools—does not sufficiently rejoice in the wonder of God's gift of creativity nor respect the patterns that have blossomed.

---

6 Gilleland, "How 'Christian' Are African Independent Churches?": 259–71.

Churches and Cultures: "The Muslim Convert Church"

What should a church look like when its members come from Muslim families? And what are best practices for such a church's outreach? In the years since *New Paths in Muslim Evangelism* was published, discussions have boiled, pages have proliferated, and developments like the insider movement and disciple-making movements have rolled out. Many of the seeds were planted in Parshall's earlier work, in chapters like "The Muslim Convert Church," "Problematic Christian Practices," "Muslim Religious Rituals," and "Muslim Social Practices."

The apostles also wrestled with these issues. The earliest churches were Jewish. Yet Acts 6 describes *Greek* widows who were neglected in the church's daily food distribution. Because of this conflict, the church appointed seven deacons. The widows were actually all Jews, some "Hebraic" Jews and others "Grecian" Jews. In the larger church, to be sure, a few non-Jewish persons were accepting Jesus as Lord, like the Ethiopian eunuch (Acts 8:26–40) and the Roman centurion Cornelius along with his family (Acts 10). So inevitably, as Gentile believers increased, the church would have to face the question: How Jewish does a Christian need to be?[7]

It was the multicultural fellowship at Antioch that precipitated this question (Acts 11:19–24; 15:1–33). Antioch was a beautiful, powerful, free-thinking city on the Mediterranean coast three hundred miles north of Jerusalem. Besides being an official Roman capitol, Antioch was a nexus for international communication. Ships sailed in from the west. Silk Road caravans arrived from the east. Turks came to trade from the north, and Arabs and Jews from the south. All brought goods and opinions and custom that simmered in the stew of Antioch. The place was also home to perhaps twenty thousand Jews, who enjoyed more rights and privileges than was the case in many cities.

Persecution had scattered the Jerusalem church. Wherever the believers went, they continued to meet for worship, teaching, and mutual aid. In free-thinking Antioch their joyful witness and the blessing of the Holy Spirit attracted many Greeks to the faith. These new believers knew very little about the Jewish law.

---

7 What to do with believing Gentiles was not a completely new issue. Throughout the centuries, some aliens had come to worship the God of Israel. They were known as *proselytes*. Male proselytes were expected to undergo circumcision, and all proselytes were expected to submit to the whole burden of the Jewish law. Even so, "It is unlikely that the proselyte ever attained in practice a real, as distinct from theoretical, equality with his Jewish-born brethren, even though Scripture and the best rabbinic teachings ordained that he should" (Stewart, "Proselyte," 1048). (Broadly welcoming Scripture texts include 1 Kgs 8:41–43; Isa 2:2–4; 49:6; 54:3–8; Jer 3:17; Zeph 3:9.) Beyond true proselytes, a second and much larger category included uncircumcised sympathizers. They worshiped and studied in the synagogues, but could not bring themselves to undergo the ritual of circumcision.

News of this reached the church in Jerusalem, and they sent Barnabas to Antioch. When he arrived and saw what the grace of God had done, he was glad and encouraged them all to remain true to the Lord with all their hearts. He was a good man, full of the Holy Spirit and faith, and a great number of people were brought to the Lord. (Acts 11:22–24 NIV)

Barnabas saw the need for an experienced Christian teacher who would feel at home with non-Jewish life, would understand the Jewish Scriptures thoroughly, and would testify to a dynamic experience with Jesus. He remembered Paul. Years before, when the newly converted Paul had come to Jerusalem, most Christians were afraid of him. But Barnabas spoke up and affirmed Paul's authentic transformation. Paul was accepted as a member in good standing (Acts 9:27). Now, thinking about Antioch's needs, Barnabas journeyed one hundred miles northwest to Tarsus and invited Paul to share in the ministry.

Time passed. The Antioch believers grew in their understanding of Scripture. Then they received a new vision. It called them to extend their witness to the Lord Jesus Christ across national and ethnic boundaries. This was in line with Abraham's commission to be a blessing to all the families of the earth (Gen 12:3), and Isaiah's portrayal of God's people as a light to the nations (Gen 42–49). The new vision resonated with Jesus' command to witness to all peoples.

You will be my witnesses in Jerusalem, and in all Judea and Samaria, and to the ends of the earth. (Acts 1:8 NIV)

Therefore go and make disciples of all nations. (Matt 28:19 NIV)

Paul in particular felt deeply for the people who had never heard the gospel. For example, in his letter to the Romans he spoke of his "obligation" to share the gospel with both Jews and Greeks (1:14–16). Concluding the letter, he mentioned his plan to evangelize in Spain, which was the outer edge of the known world: "It has always been my ambition to preach the gospel where Christ was not known" (15:20 NIV).

Returning to the time and situation regarding the earliest Gentile believers, Paul and Barnabas consulted the elders in Jerusalem and "presented to them the gospel that I preach among the Gentiles" (Gal 2:2 NIV). Regarding the elders, Paul said, "they recognized that I had been entrusted with the task of preaching the gospel to the uncircumcised, just as Peter had been to the circumcised... James, Cephas and John, those esteemed as pillars, gave me and Barnabas the right hand of fellowship when they recognized the grace given to me. They agreed that we should go to the Gentiles, and they to the circumcised." (Gal 2:7, 9 NIV).

In time, the Holy Spirit told the leaders of the church in Antioch, "Set apart for me Barnabas and Saul for the work to which I have called them" (Acts 13:2 NIV). Taking time to fast and pray, the church sensed a confirmation. Then they blessed the two men and watched them head out, "sent on their way by the Holy Spirit" (Acts 13:4 NIV).

When Barnabas and Paul came to a new city, their first stop was generally the local synagogue. Here they spoke about Jesus as the completion of all that the Jews hoped for. After that, they would expand their witness to citizens of diverse backgrounds. People of all types believed, and both small and large fellowship groups were formed. Finally, having planted the church in numerous places, the pair headed home to their base in Antioch.

> From Attalia they sailed back to Antioch, where they had been committed to the grace of God for the work they had now completed. On arriving there, they gathered the church together and reported all that God had done through them and how he had opened a door of faith to the Gentiles. And they stayed there a long time with the disciples. (Acts 14:26–28 NIV)

Criticism was seething in the larger church, however. Gentile-dominated worship groups worried traditional Jewish believers, especially when these new groups omitted so much of the law that had guided God's people down through the centuries. Moses had transmitted the law and cautioned the people never to let it go. Josiah had found the law after it had been lost during evil times, and with its help led the community to a new start. Ezra read the law to all the people, and then made sure it was explained in Aramaic, their spoken language. Jesus himself said that not one jot of the law would be erased (Matt 5:17–19). So how could Paul and Barnabas treat the law so casually? And what about circumcision? God personally had initiated that rite with Abraham. It was the key mark of God's people.

> Certain people came down from Judea and were teaching the believers, "Unless you are circumcised, according to the custom taught by Moses, you cannot be saved." (Acts 15:1 NIV)

Today such questions continue to boil. Should believers from Muslim background keep the fast of Ramadan, or must they give that up? May they pray five times daily at set times, facing toward Mecca? May they read the Quran regularly, or recite certain key chapters of worship to the Creator? May they continue to attend the mosque? Should they call themselves "Muslims who follow Jesus as Lord"?

Illustrating the importance of culture in the church community, Parshall outlined some differences between Muslim-background and Hindu-background followers of Jesus in South Asia.[8] The first believers in this region

8 Parshall, *New Paths in Muslim Evangelism.*

came from Hindu families. Unwittingly, they drew on that heritage as they developed Christian terms and practices. Some of these elements were (and are) offensive to Muslims, and to Muslim-background believers, who often identify Hindu-related words and acts as idolatrous. Such practices had no place in the worship of the one God, the Muslims felt. Even simple ethnically specific words and acts could be alienating. The contrasts were extensive. Here are some examples:

1. The Hindu word *nomoskar* is a common form of greeting for Christians. (The Muslims use *a salam oalaikum.*)
2. *Iswar* is the Hindu and Christian term for God. (*Allah* is the word used by Muslims.)
3. *Boli dan* is the word of Hindu and Christian communities to denote offering of a sacrifice. (*Korbani* is used by Muslims.)
4. The Hindu word *babu* rather than the Muslim *sahib* is used by Christians as a title for a male.
5. The complete Christian vocabulary for relatives is Hindu.
6. Christian names are often taken directly from Hindu. Some Western and biblical names are used also.
7. The word *puja* is used by Hindus to denote the worship of their idols. The same word is frequently used by Christians in their songs and prayers to denote worship of God the Father and Jesus the Son.[9]

Many Hindu practices are also found in the church:

1. The uniquely Hindu *dhuti* (five yards of material wrapped around the body) is worn by many village Christian men. (It is never worn by a Muslim.)
2. Very few Hindu and Christian males have beards. (Beards are common among Muslims.)
3. Christians, like Hindus, fold their hands in greetings. (Muslims salute.)
4. Christians and Hindus do not circumcise their sons. (Muslims do.)
5. The eating habits of Christians and Hindus are very similar. They both eat pork (which is repugnant to Muslims). Most Christians abstain from beef, as do Hindus. Christians and Hindus eat their lentils and rice before their meat and vegetables. (Muslims eat their meat and vegetables first.)
6. *Annaprashan* is a celebration of feeding a child his first rice—a unique ceremony observed only by Hindus and Christians.
7. Drama and musicals are used by both Hindus and Christians to communicate religious teaching. (Muslims do not sing or have instruments in their mosque services).

---

9 Ibid., 47-48.

Such contrasts can sow confusion and even distrust between believers. How much do Jesus' people need to change their customs? When should we confront our culture and when should we adapt with appreciation? That was the issue faced by the church in Antioch when "certain people came down from Judea to Antioch and were teaching the believers, 'Unless you are circumcised, according to the custom taught by Moses, you cannot be saved'" (Acts 15:1 NIV).

Paul and Barnabas opposed this strongly. They felt that Jewish customs, specifically circumcision, should *not* be required for believers from other cultures. "This brought Paul and Barnabas into sharp dispute and debate with them" (Acts 15:2 NIV).

In the end, a conference was convened in Jerusalem. Paul and Barnabas were sent as delegates from the Antioch church. Traveling south by way of Phoenicia and Samaria, they shared with believers along the way "how the Gentiles had been converted. This news made all the believers very glad" (Acts 15:3 NIV). Once in Jerusalem, they were welcomed by the apostles and elders "to whom they reported everything God had done through them" (Acts 15:4 NIV).

Then the formal arguments began. Must the Gentiles be circumcised and obey the law of Moses? After much discussion, Peter stood up. He himself had a complex history with this issue. On one hand, a vision had directed Peter to the home of a God-fearing Roman centurion named Cornelius. When Peter shared the gospel there, the household believed! The Spirit directed Peter to baptize them (without circumcision) and—even more shocking to his mind— to eat with them foods that had been banned by Mosaic law (Acts 10). When Christian leaders asked Peter to justify his actions, he simply told the story and pointed out the obvious presence of the Holy Spirit in the new disciples.

On another occasion, Peter was faced with this issue again. This time Peter was visiting Antioch and enjoying the integrated fellowship meals there. Some traditional Jewish believers from Judea arrived. To avoid upsetting the visitors, Peter moved to a separate table and began to eat with the Jewish believers apart from the Greeks. Other Jewish-background Christians joined him, even Barnabas (Gal 2:11–13).

Paul erupted. In front of everybody, Paul blasted Peter for not living in line with the liberating truth of the gospel:

> You are a Jew, yet you live like a Gentile and not like a Jew. How is it, then, that you force Gentiles to follow Jewish customs?

> We who are Jews by birth and not sinful Gentiles know that a person is not justified by the works of the law, but by faith in Jesus Christ. So we, too, have put our faith in Christ Jesus that we may be justified by faith in Christ and

not by the works of the law, because by the works of the law no one will be justified.... .

For through the law I died to the law so that I might live for God. I have been crucified with Christ and I no longer live, but Christ lives in me. The life I now live in the body, I live by faith in the Son of God, who loved me and gave himself for me. I do not set aside the grace of God, for if righteousness could be gained through the law, Christ died for nothing! (Gal 2:14–16, 19–21 NIV)

So when Peter stood up to speak to the Jerusalem Council, he was carrying all this baggage. What would he say? He spoke simply:

Brothers, you know that some time ago God made a choice among you that the Gentiles might hear from my lips the message of the gospel and believe. God, who knows the heart, showed that he accepted them by giving the Holy Spirit to them, just as he did to us.... . Now then, why do you try to test God by putting on the necks of Gentiles a yoke that neither we nor our ancestors have been able to bear? No! We believe it is through the grace of our Lord Jesus that we are saved, just as they are. (Acts 15:7–8, 10–11 NIV)

James, who was the brother of Jesus, was the recognized leader at the Council. Eventually he took the floor in order to draw the diverse views together. In contrast to Paul's emphasis on faith alone, James was known for insisting that good works were vital. In his letter, which was possibly written before the Jerusalem Council, James asked:

What good is it, my brothers and sisters, if someone claims to have faith but has no deeds? Can such faith save them?...You see that a person is considered righteous by what they do and not by faith alone. (James 2:14, 24 NIV)

Would James require "deeds of the law" from the new believers? No, the good works he urged were deeds of charity rather than legal or ritual acts (James 1:27; 2:14–26; 3:13–17; 5:1–6). Therefore James outlined a compromise. In regard to the Gentiles coming to God, he drew on the heritage of the Jewish Scriptures, especially the prophet Amos. Then James made simple recommendations. Circumcision was nowhere on his list. His recommendations were approved and documented in an elegantly written letter which was sent to the church in Antioch, and undoubtedly circulated well beyond that city.

How much contextualization is appropriate for a congregation of believers from non-Christian backgrounds? Where does contextualization slide into syncretism? This issue continues to reverberate. On the one hand, we want churches that worship in local ways, connected to local values. On the other hand, we don't want to dilute or pollute the gospel. That was the Jerusalem Council's concern, it was Parshall's concern, and it is also ours.

Globalization and Cultures

Today a new issue has arisen: Globalization threatens cultural distinctives. People text from everywhere to everywhere. All over the world citizens watch many of the same blockbuster movies, know the names of the same actors, hum the same songs. On TV and online they view material things—clothing, electronic devices, recreational accoutrements—and find these desirable. They observe styles of social interaction different from those of their heritage, and these new patterns look exciting and empowering. Many have kin employed in richer countries who send money back home, funding businesses, houses, education, and novel consumption patterns. Those kin also send home stories of new ways of living.

Anthropologist Michael Rynkiewich offers this definition of globalization:

> Globalization is the widespread engagement of people with an expanding worldwide system of communication, commerce, and culture that is producing broad uniformities across selected sectors of many societies, as well as generating multiple hybrid cultures in various stages of reception, rejection, and reinvention of innovations.[10]

Where are the unique cultures today? They seem to be submerged under a flood of globalization. In such a world, maybe the issues of Acts 15 are irrelevant. Maybe efforts to adapt are no longer necessary as the world gets "smaller." Who truly cares anymore? Aren't cultural differences eroding? In any case, shouldn't we, within the church, try to love one other and minimize our cultural contrasts?

Yet globalization is not enough. Specifically, it is not human enough. Rynkiewich adds, "Globalization commodifies everything."[11] Even secular scholars recognize that contemporary people continue to need cultures, because we are not merely animals, or robots, or producers, or consumers—we are persons who are parts of communities with heritages.

For example, anthropologist Clifford Geertz observes, "Even when our material needs are met, still our motivation ... emotional resilience ... and moral strength ... must come from somewhere, from some vision of public purpose anchored in a compelling image of social reality."[12] Being a world citizen is too vague to provide this motivation and strength, according to Geertz. World citizenship makes the common person feel insignificant. Even national citizenship may breed apathy. But when you are a member of an ethnic group, you have celebrations which give zest, values which give a cognitive framework,

---

10 Rynkiewich, *Soul, Self, and Society*, 234.
11 Ibid., 235.
12 Geertz, "After the Revolution," 70.

action patterns which give direction to your days, and associational ties which root you in a human context. You have a place in time in the universe, a base for the conviction that you are part of the continuity of life flowing from the past and pulsing on into the future. You are in the story.

There are rhythms to living in this world. These are expressed locally, through specific cultural patterns. They cannot be known at the abstract, global level. Disciplining a child, for example, is not virtual. Being fired from a job is not a media experience. Having a baby is not a game. Coping with cancer is not abstract. Global systems may immerse us in virtual realities—media, packaged music, the stock market, sports scores, and news flashes—in which great tragedies are juxtaposed with beer ads. Yet if we are absorbed in the global or virtual level, we miss out on the real rhythms of nature and society. Seed time and harvest, and the health of our soil, trees, and water. Friendship, courtship, marriage, parenting, aging, and dying.

New York Times columnist Thomas Friedman explores this in *The Lexus and the Olive Tree,* where the Lexus represents the global economy and the olive tree represents particular local cultures. The Lexus is never enough.

We need the olive tree too.[13] Manuel Castells, in *The Rise of the Networked Society,* argues that although a networked globe means an integration of power, this happens on a level increasingly divorced from our personal lives. He calls it "structural schizophrenia."[14]

This applies even among the diasporas that move by the millions from one land to another. The second generation may not speak their parents' language. They may chafe at their parents' traditions. Their worldviews and behaviors may be quite different. In the face of such changes, we cannot "essentialize" cultures as though they always stayed the same. On the other hand, even when a culture changes, a thread of the heritage continues. Even among second and third generation immigrants, some of the components of ethnic identity will characterize them, such as:

- self-ascription as member of a shared ethnic community;
- other-ascription regarding members of an ethnic community;
- shared ancestral land and language;
- shared history, stories of suffering, and heroes;
- behaviors appropriate between close kin;
- holidays and humor.

Cultures still matter. Generation X and Generation Y mission workers must pay attention, because they are driven to getting results fast. This compounds

---

13 Friedman, *The Lexus and the Olive Tree.*
14 Castells, *The Rise of the Networked Society,* 459.

the American tendency to charge full steam ahead—and inadvertently trample over other cultures in the process. Defining problems pragmatically, we aim for quick, measurable solutions. Ten houses built. Ten preaching points. Twenty Bible studies. One hundred people won to Christ. We approach mission through systems management, diagramming strategy concepts such as nonresident missionaries, multi-individual decision-making units, church planting movements (CPMs), disciple making movements (DMMs), or criteria to distinguish unreached peoples.

Because we are goal-oriented, we screen out imponderables that do not fit our planning procedures, especially if we have to discuss them in another language. Efficiency matters. Our donors expect it. Unfortunately, this means we sometimes run right over local people without taking time to hear their gentle objections or read their body language. Instead of pausing to appreciate our mutual humanity, we objectify them as problems, and ask, "How can we fix you?" We reduce them to labels so we can move forward with our ministry projects. Unconsciously we fear that if we really interacted with their complexity, it would slow us down.

It does take time to learn a language, to adapt to a way of life, to be a friend. It requires openness to ambiguity and even to failure. It is much more than superficial mouthings about multiculturalism. If we are going to absorb the historic continuity, the connotative richness, and the contextual integration of a culture, it will be hard work. To honor that culture, we will have to die a little to our own ways of thinking and acting. Like a seed falling into the ground, we may find it dark and uncomfortable. But in time we will be reborn like a sprout, like a blossom. At first we will be fragile, ignorant, and incompetent, almost helpless. We will have to practice and repeat, over and over, like a toddler. If, however, we are willing to go through the death and rebirth that is part of adapting to a culture, the yield in God's good time may be a hundred-fold—brothers and sisters and fathers and mothers.

Sensitivity to culture matters. Reflections from Alaska, Borneo, and Kenya will illustrate this. Two years ago I was in the Alaska State Museum, marveling at intricate ivory, fur, stone, basketry, sealskin, wood, fabric, and other artifacts. Silently I was praising God for his gift of creativity to Alaskan native peoples. Then my praise was jarred by an audio tape playing behind me. "Missionaries destroyed Alaskan cultural treasures," the voice asserted, and went on to elaborate that theme. My heart sank. If an Inuit or Aleut or Athabascan listened to that, what would they think of the gospel? How careful we need to be not to marginalize or minimize or quickly judge other cultures, lest we reinforce the broad stereotyping that I heard on that audio tape.

In Borneo, by contrast, I saw how Christianity rescued a culture from annihilation. The Lun Bawang and Kelabit peoples were jungle dwellers who hunted forest rhinoceros (before they became endangered), picked fruits from vines sixty feet above the forest floor, and rode white water rapids to trade and visit. European colonial rule destabilized them. Alcohol flooded into their communities. Drunkenness and family violence exploded. Then three Australians felt the call to bring the gospel to these people.

"Your goals are admirable," the Borneo officials told the missionaries when they arrived. "Unfortunately, it is not worth your while to travel up those mountains. That society is so badly disintegrating that those people are going to disappear. Yes, it's a tragedy, but that's just the way it is. It's inevitable. And yes, that language is going to die out, too."

However, the missionaries travelled into the interior, learned the language, and shared the gospel. The people responded, experienced transformation of life, quit drinking, asked the government for schools, and became contributing citizens. Today if they are asked, some will say, "If not for the gospel, our people would be gone. It's because of the gospel that we are still here, as well as our language and culture. The gospel challenged the evils in our culture, but it did not destroy it. It kept our heritage alive. We are a people today because of the gospel."

A third example comes from Kenya. Wanjiru Gitau's award-winning book, *Megachurch Christianity Reconsidered: Millennials and Social Change in African Perspective*, faces the intersection of the local with the global. In African cities like Nairobi there are many cosmopolitan, educated people who aspired to be middle-class. Although quite a few have grown up in the church, they have dropped out, because they see church as old-fashioned and out of touch with current life. Extended family and tribal customs are shrugged off, too, since they also limit freedom. To find community, these cosmopolitans cluster in nightclubs.

A church named Mavuno Chapel saw these cosmopolitans—future leaders of society—as sheep without a shepherd. Mavuno tailored an outreach to them. Music was key. A Mavuno church band began performing one Saturday night a month at a dinner club called the Carnivore. The church went where the people were and communicated in a genre they understood. Eventually they identified the band with the church and invited the audience to a weekly service tailored to them. Over time the band cultivated friendships with various artists and musicians. Quite a few came to faith and began creating music for the Lord in their own genres.

To find the right music, the Mavuno band tapped into contemporary African-American gospel music. At that time—the 1990s—Nairobi's airwaves were experiencing an influx of Western music. The lyrics were often sexual and disrespectful, but the music was highly popular. Meanwhile, local Christian radio featured white Western/global musicians. In both the general and the Christian media, music seemed to be losing touch with African culture. But "Afro-American gospel music is rooted in an experiential expression of faith, and thus is more emotive, energetic, and community-oriented than the mellow, vertically-focused white music," according to Gitau.[15]

At the Carnivore, the church band performed "Afro neo soul music, a lyrical fusion of Nairobi urban storytelling and American rhythm and blues."[16] They also created new music in this style. This was very well received. The local culture was honored, yet also enriched by the global. African cultural patterns were resurrected, reinvigorated, and treasured, even among these modern and cosmopolitan Kenyans.

Only One Offense

We live in a decade different from the one in which Phil Parshall wrote *New Paths in Muslim Evangelism*. Yet adaptation has never been more important than now, because we live in fast times. We want immediate results and successes. To get those, we are tempted to treat people as projects, as things, forgetting that true human growth takes time. It still takes nine months to grow a baby. You can't crowd-fund it and have it here next week. It takes time to grow a reliable friendship. It takes time to grow a holy life.

Parshall advocated taking the time to appreciate cultures. "How many boards today encourage their missionaries to adapt … appreciative of the target culture?" he pled.[17] Cultural adaptation mattered to him, even if it meant giving up pork. Only one offense should intrude: the true offense of the gospel, the cross that is a scandal and stumbling block to people's pride in every culture. Beyond that, Christian witnesses should adapt. We do this because God created the potential for culture and delights in its variation. We adapt because Jesus immersed himself in a local culture. We adapt because the apostles recognized that the Holy Spirit indwells people in all sorts of cultures. We adapt because human beings need heritage communities even during times of dynamic change. We adapt so that around the throne at the end of time, we may praise God through our diversity, as celebrated in the words of theologian Justo Gonzalez:

---

15 Gitau, *Megachurch Christianity Reconsidered: Millennials and Social Change in African Perspective*, 119.
16 Ibid., 71.
17 Parshall, *New Paths*, 99.

On that great waking up morning when the stars begin to fall, when we gather at the river where angel feet have trod, we shall all, from all nations and tribes and peoples and languages, we shall all sing without ceasing, "Holy, Holy, Holy! All the saints adore Thee, casting down our golden crowns before the glassy sea, cherubim and seraphim, Japanese and Swahili, American and European, Cherokee and Ukrainian, falling down before Thee, who wert, and art, and evermore shall be! Amen."[18]

References

Bragg, R. 1997. *All Over But the Shoutin'*. New York: Vintage Books.

Castells, M. 1996. *The Rise of the Networked Society*. London: Blackwell Publishers.

Friedman, T. 1999. *The Lexus and the Olive Tree*. New York: Farrar, Straus, Giroux.

Gadjigo, S. 1993. *Ousmane Sembene: Dialogues with Critics and Writers*. Amherst, MA: University of Massachusetts Press.

Geertz, C. 1973. "After the Revolution: The Fate of Nationalism in the New States," in *The Interpretation of Cultures*. New York: Basic Books.

Gilleland, D. 1986. "How 'Christian' Are African Independent Churches?" *Missiology* 14 (3): 259–72.

Gitau, W. 2018. *Megachurch Christianity Reconsidered: Millennials and Social Change in African Perspective*. Downers Grove, IL: InterVarsity.

Gonzalez, J. 1999. *For the Healing of the Nations*. New York: Orbis Books.

Parshall, P. 1980. *New Paths in Muslim Evangelism*. Grand Rapids: Baker.

Rynkiewich, M. 2011. *Soul, Self, and Society: A Postmodern Anthropology for Mission in a Postcolonial World*. Eugene, OR: Cascade Books.

Stewart, R. A. 1962. "Proselyte," in *New Bible Dictionary*. Edited by J. D. Douglas. Grand Rapids: Eerdmans.

Stockdale, A. A. 1964. "God Left the Challenge in the Earth." *His*, 20.

---

18 Gonzalez, *For the Healing of the Nations*, 111–12.

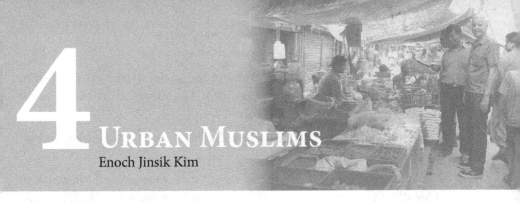

4 URBAN MUSLIMS

Enoch Jinsik Kim

Holding Multiple Memberships

This chapter represents an effort to expand the passion for Muslims and the contextual ministry of Phil Parshall toward contemporary urban Muslims. I will lay the theoretical framework with social network theory and evangelism theory in order to understand the identity confusion experienced by Muslims who become followers of Jesus. They negotiate their identities as a coping mechanism to simultaneously protect themselves and guard their new faith. Such negotiation phenomena are witnessed in the lives of Muslim background believers (MBBs) and in the lives of contemporary urbanites. I refer to these people as "multiple membership holders." As multiple membership holders, urban Muslims often prefer to stay in the so-called fuzzy zone, a third category, rather than fully embracing either of the two faiths.

Introduction

When I was training for missions before setting off on a journey to interact with Chinese Muslims, I questioned, "Why would a missionary from a Far East Asian country with less than two hundred years of Christian history request forgiveness from Muslims for the Crusades that occurred a thousand years prior?" I was an Asian missionary who had lived practically without regard for Muslims, not regarding the Western burden of guilt from ancestral transgressions; but I was liberated from the confusion by Phil Parshall and his research focused on contextualization. By revealing the massive love and humility to help just one Muslim become a follower of Christ, Parshall's research helped me to turn my attention to the Muslims in front of me. If I were to summarize Parshall's research, I would cite Paul: "We do not cause trouble for those … who are turning to God" (Acts 15:19 NASB), and "I have become all things to all people" (1 Cor 9:22 NASB).

This chapter, as a part of this Festschrift for Phil Parshall, was written from perspectives within the field of sociology. Building upon Parshall's legacy and contribution to missiology, I will examine the social dynamics of Muslims turning to Christ in rapidly changing cities. Accordingly, I will address the following questions:

1. What impact does the change in the social network of city dwellers have on the identity of Muslims?

2. What missiological implications do evangelists face regarding the negotiation of identity that occurs when Muslims convert from Islam to following Jesus?

Urban Muslims' Social Network and Value Changes

A city is not only a place where many people live but also a place where people are transformed by social networking. Because urban areas are heavily populated, individuals have opportunities to meet and socialize with more diverse people groups where they can better understand the Other, and become influenced by them. This is particularly relevant in the ministry of Muslim evangelism.

Changes in social networks also greatly impact Muslim evangelism. Social networks are channels for sharing information; and "the gospel is good news" means the gospel functions as information to be shared. That is why the gospel, like other news, flows through the channels of relationships and media. In other words, the gospel is intended to flow through human networks.[1] For this reason, understanding social networks and information channels should significantly impact the process of sharing the gospel with Muslims.

Sociologists divide human networks into ascribed relationships, primary networks, achieved relationships, and secondary networks, based on the intimacy of people and their social proximity.[2] The primary network is an innate or naturally created relationship, like a blood relationship.[3] Conversely, the secondary network refers to relationships that are obtained from a social life with friends, colleagues, or acquaintances. Contrary to the primary network (you can't choose your family), the secondary network is based on choices people make.

Just as most people who live in cities engage in diverse relationships, urban Muslims possess a much more diverse secondary network than Muslims in traditional societies.[4] This is why urban Muslims are typically able to interact with more diverse groups, classes, and distant people. After all, Muslims in cities experience tremendous changes because of the diversity of their secondary social networks.

---

1 Smith, *Creating Understanding*, 144–80.
2 McCarty, "Structure in Personal Networks," 8; Wasserman and Faust, *Social Network Analysis*, 8.
3 Bohannan, *Social Anthropology*, 55; Eames and Goode, *Anthropology of the City*, chapter 4.
4 Eames states that urban social networks have more choices of contact. Eames and Goode, *Anthropology of the City*, 157.

Urban Muslims Are Multiple Membership Holders

Today, most people are living within multiple groups within their homes and societies. Hence, they engage in a variety of roles and positions. For example, my friend Ahmet is a schoolteacher. He is the head of his family, and when he goes to the mosque, he is a translation volunteer who translates a standard language into a minority language. Humans have probably always engaged in this sort of multifunctionality. However, due to increasingly complex secondary networks and social environments, Muslims naturally have begun to undertake more diverse roles and positions. Many contemporary Muslims belong to much more diverse groups than Ahmet does, finding diversity in their work cultures, secondary jobs, hobbies, neighborhood and community organizations, and even online communities. To effectively participate in each group, they find it is essential to establish different identities for each group, as identity is made and refined within social relations.[5]

Identity is created by roles, the groups a person belongs to, and the tendency (personality) expressed by individuals.[6] Additionally, identity is created within the surrounding relationships and contexts of society.[7] People discover and build their own identities within social activities. For this reason, typical social activities are only possible when different personas are displayed in different contexts. Therefore, everyone possesses multiple identities within their social lives. It is as if Ahmet appears with different appropriate personas, such as teacher, head of a family, and translator, at each appropriate place.

Various researchers, including those from the fields of psychology[8] and sociology,[9] have conducted numerous studies on the multiple identities phenomenon. Ethnological studies by Paul Spickard, among others, focusing on immigrants to Europe, are notable.[10] In their books, Spickard and other authors utilized similar jargon to supplement multiple identities, including transnational subjectivities, translocational positionalities,[11] doing belonging,[12] symbolic ethnicity,[13] and instrumental ethnicity.[14] Their consistent argument remains that identity is not fixed; rather, it is an ongoing process.[15] This is because a person's identity is developed by so much more than their genetics

---

5   Stryker, *Symbolic Interactionism.*
6   Burke and Stets, *Identity Theory*, 112–29.
7   Ibid., 3.
8   Gergen, "Multiple Identity"; James, *The Principles of Psychology.*
9   Horowitz, "Ethnic Identity," 118; Baskauskas, "Multiple Identities"
10 Spickard, *Multiple Identities.*
11 Rastas, "Ethnic Identities and Transnational Subjectivities."
12 Gunnarsson, "Doing Belonging: Young Women of Middle Eastern Backgrounds in Sweden."
13 Gans, "Symbolic Ethnicity"; Westerlung-Cook, "Intercountry Adoption."
14 Colombo and Rebughini, "The Children of Immigrants in Italy," 209.
15 Okitikpi, *Working with Children of Mixed Parentage*, 183.

and ethnicity. Identity is more closely related to relationships and behaviors within the social environment. In other words, constantly changing an identity is natural because a person has a social identity and an ascribed identity.

The term "multiple identities" is used differently in many academic disciplines, and thus it can confuse people. In psychology, "multiple identities" describes schizophrenia or identity confusion.[16] However, Spickard and others argued that normal people adopt and use multiple identities naturally without being confused by who they are.[17] This is possible because there is a "control tower" that directs identity in cases of multiple identities.[18] This control tower organizes various identities within a hierarchy so one can undertake a proper role and position with each social interaction.

Another metaphor for the control tower would be the ways people situationally decide to remove the appropriate membership card to different establishments from their wallets. Accordingly, each membership card within the wallet functions as a persona but does not completely define a person. Rather, the self can be considered as being akin to the control tower. Just because one of my membership cards presents the persona of a body builder who works out at 24 Hour Fitness doesn't mean I can be completely defined as a healthy person. I have two membership cards to ice cream parlors.

To avert the confusion of terms like "multiple identities" and other ambiguous terms, when I speak of the struggle MBBs face, I use the term "membership holders." Hopefully this term more appropriately describes the multiple identities of contemporary people.

Like others, Muslims in the city are individuals who hold multiple memberships in the control tower. The environment of the city forces them to join diverse groups. For their survival and career development, they often participate in groups that are totally unrelated to religion or their cultural or familial background. These urban Muslims express a distinctly Muslim persona at home in the morning, then traverse multiple personas throughout the day that may not even relate to their religion or heritage, only to return to their Muslim persona at the close of the day.

Urban Muslims Negotiate Their Identit(ies)

When people belong to two different communities, they may face conflict, and even experience identity confusion. For example, Tim Green related the

---

16 Clausen and Kohn, "Relation of Schizophrenia to the Social Structure of a Small City"; Lofland, *Deviance and Identity.*
17 Gergen, "Multiple Identity," 31–35.
18 Burke and Stets, *Identity Theory,* 133–40.

words of a Pakistani MBB who said, "I have to show myself in both circles.... . I have to show myself as a Muslim [among Muslims] and among Christians, as a Christian."[19]

I personally experienced this growing up in a strong Confucian family. I was required to live a double life after I began to follow Jesus. While I had a sweet time with my brothers and sisters at church every weekend, I spent much time engaging in ancestral rites and conforming to Confucian culture and worldviews for the sake of my immediate and extended family.

Like the Pakistani MBB, holders of multiple memberships may suffer from identity confusion while actually spending more time efficiently and creatively portraying different identities.[20] Essentially, they are negotiating their identities.[21] Negotiating identity is a person's effort to identify and present the right persona in the right place at the right time. Drawing on multiple cultural identities does not mean one is deficient in the culture of heritage; rather, it means he or she knows how to navigate various cultures. An example of such a negotiation is exemplified in the case of immigrants who migrate to more developed countries.[22] In fact, this phenomenon of identity negotiation is naturally observed among all people living within a complex contemporary society.

Yet negotiating identities sometimes leads to serious problems. This is because the persona shown in one place is not easily identifiable in other urban settings.

Models of Discipling MBBs

Traditionally, Christians have tried to understand how Muslims followed Jesus by using Western regeneration and spiritual growth concepts. Alternatively, they may consider engaging in power evangelism through miracles and dreams. If only these two models are applied to Muslim holders of multiple memberships, what would we miss? Furthermore, what are the dynamics that are unique when Muslims follow Jesus? I think the phenomena of holding multiple identities and of negotiating identity can answer these questions. But first, I will critique two traditional models of evangelism.

Spiritual Growth: The Process Model Based on Ordo Salutis

For a long time, Western churches have conceptualized a person's journey of faith by the principle of *Ordo Salutis*.[23] *Ordo Salutis* is a theory that argues a

---

19 Green, "Identity Choices at the Border Zone," 54.
20 Wallman, "Identity Options," 74.
21 Burke and Stets, *Identity Theory*, 136–39, 185–86.
22 Gunnarsson, "Doing Belonging," 109; Mukazhanova, "The Politics of Multiple Identities in Kazakhstan."
23 Berkhof, *Christian Faith*, 378.

person's faith matures through stages, and that every stage of maturity involves the intervention of the Holy Spirit. This theory, as a kind of process theory, is described as a concept that, as time goes on, the disciples of Christ advance to the next level as they become more spiritually mature. Recently, with the help of student mission organizations and discipleship training movements, the first step toward becoming a disciple of Christ has been conceptualized as beginning with repentance in order to receive Jesus and then advancing through the stages of maturity to the final stage of sanctification. So, repentance was the beginning of the process.

And in fact, missionaries working in the Islamic world often try to engage in discipleship using the process model. The problem with the process model is that starting the discipleship journey with *repentance* in an Islamic context, where hostility to Christianity is usually present, can lead to significant misunderstanding. This is because the steps of planting seeds and germination cannot begin until the rocks and thorns are removed from the soil.

The process theory introduced by James Engel[24] and Viggo Søgaard[25] overcame many of these shortcomings. They believed that a person's religious maturity is not the first step of regeneration and repentance but comes after a person shifts from serious misunderstanding and hostility to less misunderstanding and hostility. Consequently, they plotted the growth of a disciple of Christ from –10 to +10 instead of from 0 to +10.[26] Engel's and Søgaard's contributions made great progress and created a new paradigm in ministry within the Islamic world, making it possible to accept moving from –7 to –6 as equally valuable as moving from 0 to +1 (wherein a person is saved).

In other words, we should not expect MBB behaviors and testimonies of conversion to be the same as those in Western society. To utilize the process theory in the Islamic context, two issues need to be supplemented in Western theories of discipleship. First, include extreme hostility in the steps, in line with Engel and Søgaard. Second, when addressing one's spiritual situation, we must not only consider one's stage but also the direction one is headed.

Upon personal observations, it appears that traditional models assume that when life begins, growth is the next natural step. However, we all know that the spiritual states often vary; some zigzag while others backtrack. I knew of quite a few Muslims who gave up their new faith and went back to their original faith, and sometimes became even more negative toward Christianity. Therefore, when examining one's spiritual state, we should also observe one's

---

24 Engel, *Contemporary Christian Communication*.
25 Søgaard, *Everything You Need to Know for a Cassette Ministry*; *Media in Church and Mission*; *Research in Church and Mission*.
26 Engel, *Getting Your Message Across*.

recent directional movement rather than solely assuming one is on a steady positive spiritual trajectory.

Power Encounters and Dreams: The Paradigm Shift Model

Unlike the process model introduced above (with its gradual stages), sometimes people rapidly change their minds when a paradigm shift occurs. According to "Muslims Tell 'Why I Chose Jesus'" by J. Dudley Woodberry and Russell G. Shubin, Muslims often come to Jesus for the assurance of salvation, as they encounter him in the Bible, and find the truth claims in Christianity to be more plausible than those of Islam. Muslims often embrace the gospel after having a powerful dream or vision of Jesus revealing himself, experiencing the love of another Christian, or understanding the revelation of God's love (something that is rather foreign to Islam) and his invitation to a personal relationship.[27]

Considering this, a significant proportion of Muslims jump to a high level at any stage, rather than simply following a gradual salvific process. This jump is possible because the gospel can create a paradigm shift in the lives of Muslims. Indeed, the elements discovered by Woodberry and Shubin are not elements that appeared suddenly in their lives, but spiritual issues that Muslims have longed for previously. That is, Jesus Christ filled the emptiness that Muslims and the Muslim community had pursued but could not fill, and, consequently, they experienced tremendous spiritual growth.

As one who has been practicing evangelism to Muslims for sixteen years, I urge missionaries to pursue ministry in anticipation of this paradigm shift. Paradigm-shift models are also a way that God uses to bring MBBs to himself. However, expecting supernatural experiences to occur by way of miracles and dreams can distort the nature of ministry. One should remember that Jesus and the apostle Paul spent most of their time evangelizing and nurturing people through ministry efforts.

The Identity Negotiation Model

When Muslims become followers of Jesus, they have already obtained the so-called sequential dual membership explained by Robert Schreiter. When a person moves to another faith, according to Schreiter, "Often the prior belief is so deeply inscribed on the culture of which the person is a member that the new identity can never completely supplant the earlier one."[28]

MBBs negotiate their identity within at least two societies as their interest in Jesus grows. There is a tremendous difference between these individuals' beliefs as followers of Jesus and the social expectation of hostility toward Jesus

---

27 Woodberry and Shubin, "Muslims Tell 'Why I Chose Jesus'", 28–33.
28 Schreiter, "Christian Identity and Interreligious Dialogue," 72.

surrounding them. Although they choose to follow Christ, the concepts of collective identity and social identity remain in their inner worlds.[29] This is akin to an individual believing in their heart, "O wretched man that I am!" (Rom 7:24 KJV), while saying in their mind, "Old things are passed away; behold, all things are become new" (2 Cor 5:17 KJV).

Of such cases, Tim Green stated that MBBs protect themselves and live a social life by using coping strategies, such as switching between different personas in various circumstances: a suppression that gives up one and chooses the other entirely, or a synthesis that mixes the two properly and designates a different persona for each situation.[30] If the two groups are likely to acknowledge their opponent, some MBBs embrace a third culture through a process called hybridization. Hybridization indicates the creation of actions and thoughts that both sides accept and by which a person does not feel greatly threatened.

Tim Greene introduced the concept of a "fuzzy zone"—a concept that describes the tendency of MBBs to belong to multiple circles without fully committing to any one of them.[31] The fuzzy zone is not just the third zone, but a zone that includes both elements. The fuzzy zone refers to a state in which new elements and the existing two elements are combined and progress to a new area. That is, from the moment MBBs take interest in Jesus, they begin a long process of moving between two lords and two or more social relationships.

The fuzzy zone can be ambiguous; and it can look suspicious to Christians who acknowledge traditional boundaries of orthodoxy, because they believe if anyone follows Jesus, old things in them are passed away: "Behold, all things are become new" (2 Cor 5:17 KJV). However, do MBBs need to become exactly like Western Christians? Or should they develop a new identity that serves Jesus?

For Muslims who are multiple membership holders, the fuzzy zone can be a free and familiar space, because the multiple membership holders are already very familiar with identifying only part of themselves within various groups. They may be in the process of finding their true self and their Master as they enter the fuzzy zone.

---

29 Green, "Conversion of the Light of Identity Theories," 44.
30 Ibid., 56–57.
31 Ibid., 60–61.

Conclusion

The multiple membership holder model poses a new challenge to the traditional categorization of believers. Today's Christians who observe this third zone (e.g., this fuzzy zone) from a distance may be in a similar position to that of the first-century Jewish Christians who observed pagans become Christians in Greek and Roman cities. The Jewish Christians hardly imagined there would be churches that spoke other languages. They couldn't have predicted how non-Jewish persons in every corner of the Roman Empire would be grafted into the family. Even if they could envision the future church, the Jewish Christians likely had a difficult time accepting the culture shift.

It is clear that the new MBBs who follow Christ negotiate at least two identities. They typically spend significant time in the fuzzy zone. Another clear observation is that Christians who imagined that they belong to a clearly defined and bounded set have criticized MBBs who live in the ambiguous zone. Despite this misunderstanding, the Gentiles were able to form a global Christianity over time.

Because of this, one should be cautious of making a hasty conclusion about what the fuzzy zone they create will look like in the future. Ralph Winter, who was cautious about making hasty conclusions, stated that Christians should "not hastily judge the level of faith of Muslim seekers"[32] when the C spectrum was in dispute.

One can more clearly address the MBBs in the fuzzy zone by using the process model. I compared three models of discipleship among MBBs. Each model deserves respect. Despite this, the process model should be centered on their spiritual growth, but it is necessary to go beyond the traditional *Ordo Salutis* in order to achieve a better understanding of the MBB's spiritual path. Therefore, the model should extend to the negative end of the spectrum, where there are rocks and thorns, instead of beginning with 0 (repentance) as the first step. The MBB ministry should not be tied to the traditional notion that one can only move in a forward direction.

The new process model can include the phenomena of paradigm shifts in the lives of MBBs as well. The Holy Spirit may transform seekers suddenly, as he did the apostle Paul, who jumped and moved to a mature level at the moment of his miraculous encounter with the risen Jesus (Acts 22:10). The revised process model also indicates one who made good progress at first and then regressed, like Demas (2 Tim 4:10). Or in the case of the apostle Paul, the paradigm shift model and power encounters explain how he was propelled to extreme maturity fairly rapidly. Through the new process model, we discover

---

32 Winter, "Going Far Enough: Taking Some Tips from the Historical Record," 667.

that the fuzzy zone is not simply located in a "no go" zone between Christians and Muslims. Rather, it is like a long continuum.

This process model has the potential for serious theological and missiological debate. For example, can we consider a Muslim man who changed his spiritual interest from –7 to –6 a follower of Christ? He continues to persecute Christians and lives as a typical Muslim, but he becomes open to biblical teaching and softens his attitude toward Christians after developing good relationships with Christian coworkers. If we can count him as a follower of Christ, how can we plot his spiritual growth, and at what stage can we address him as a regenerated believer?

Perhaps our knowledge of Muslim evangelism is too limited at this point to fully understand this "fuzzy zone"; but as the cases of MBBs grow, we will have more experience and data to solve this puzzle. For this reason, it is necessary to return to the basics and continue the difficult work of evangelism and fostering nurturing environments.

Postscript

The inspiration and passion for the MBB community demonstrated by Phil Parshall became an impetus for this chapter. At the beginning of this chapter, I questioned why the Crusades of one thousand years ago, which had nothing to do with me as an Asian missionary, should be an issue requiring forgiveness today. However, similar arrogance and mistakes of modern Western missionaries, which Phil Parshall confessed in his book *Beyond the Mosque*,[33] exist in the hearts of Asian missionaries in their ignorance of Muslim persons. Furthermore, Parshall showed us in his book *Muslim Evangelism* that Asian and Western missionaries could meet together under the rubric of contextualization. His enthusiasm for evangelism gave direct insight to this chapter.[34]

References

Baskauskas, L. 1977. "Multiple Identities: Adjusted Lithuanian Refugees in Los Angeles." *Urban Anthropology* 6, (2): 141–54.

Berkhof, H. 1979. *Christian Faith: An Introduction to the Study of the Faith.* Grand Rapids: Eerdmans.

Bohannan, P. 1963. *Social Anthropology.* New York: Holt Rinehart and Winston.

Burke, P. J., and J. E. Stets. 2009. *Identity Theory.* Oxford: Oxford University Press.

Clausen, J. A, and M. L. Kohn. 1959. "Relation of Schizophrenia to the Social Structure of a Small City." In *Epidemiology of Mental Disorder*, edited by B. Pasamaneck, 69–94. Washington, DC: American Association for the Advancement of Science.

33 Parshall, *Beyond the Mosque*, 177–86.
34 Parshall, *Muslim Evangelism*, 171–94.

Colombo, E., and P. Rebughini. 2013. "The Children of Immigrants in Italy: A New Generation of Italians?" In *Multiple Identities: Migrants, Ethnicity, and Membership*, edited by P. Spickard. Bloomington, IN: Indiana University Press.

Eames, E., and J. Goode. 1977. *Anthropology of the City: An Introduction to Urban Anthropology*. Prentice-Hall Series in Anthropology. Englewood Cliffs, NJ: Prentice-Hall.

Engel, J. F. 1979. *Contemporary Christian Communications*. Nashville, New York: Thomas Nelson.

———. 1989. *Getting Your Message Across*. Mandalunyong Metro Manila: OMF Literature.

Gans, H. J. 1979. "Symbolic Ethnicity: The Future of Ethnic Groups and Cultures in America." *Ethnic and Racial Studies* 2 (1): 1–20.

Gergen, K. 1972. "Multiple Identity: The Healthy, Happy Human Being Wears Many Masks," *Psychology Today* 12 (May): 31–35.

Green, T. 2013. "Conversion of the Light of Identity Theories," In *Longing for Community: Church, Ummah, or Somewhere in Between?* edited by David Greenlee. Pasadena, CA: William Carey Library.

———. 2013b "Identity Choices at the Border Zone." In *Longing for Community: Church, Ummah, or Somewhere in Between?* edited by David Greenlee. Pasadena, CA: William Carey Library.

Gunnarsson, S. 2013. "Doing Belonging: Young Women of Middle Eastern Backgrounds in Sweden." In *Multiple Identities: Migrants, Ethnicity, and Membership*, edited by P. Spickard, 88–110. Bloomington, IN: Indiana University Press.

Horowitz, D. L., 1975. "Ethnic Identity." In *Ethnicity*, edited by Nathan Glazer and Daniel Moynihan. Cambridge, MA: Harvard University Press.

James, W. 1950. *The Principles of Psychology*. New York: Dover Publications.

Lofland, J. 1969. *Deviance and Identity*. Englewood Cliffs, NJ: Prentice-Hall.

McCarty, C. 2002. "Structure in Personal Networks." *Journal of Social Structure* (3).

Mukazhanova, K. 2013. "The Politics of Multiple Identities in Kazakhstan: Current Issues and New Challenges." In *Multiple Identities: Migrants, Ethnicity, and Membership*, edited by P. Spickard, 88–113. Bloomington, IN: Indiana University Press.

Okitikpi, T. 2005. *Working with Children of Mixed Parentage*, Lyme Regis, UK: Russell House.

Parshall, P. 1985. *Beyond the Mosque: Christians within Muslim Community*. Grand Rapids: Baker.

———. 2003. *Muslim Evangelism: Contemporary Approaches to Contextualization*. Waynesboro, GA: Gabriel Publishing.

Rastas, A. 2013. "Ethnic Identities and Transnational Subjectivities." In *Multiple Identities: Migrants, Ethnicity, and Membership*, edited by P. Spickard, 45–49. Bloomington, IN: Indiana University Press.

Schreiter, R. 1994. "Christian Identity and Interreligious Dialogue." *Studies in Interreligious Dialogue* (41).

Smith, D. K. 1992. *Creating Understanding: A Handbook for Christian Communication across Cultural Landscapes*. Grand Rapids: Zondervan.

Spickard, P. 2013. *Multiple Identities: Migrants, Ethnicity, and Membership*. Bloomington, IN: Indiana University Press.

Søgaard, V., ed. 1975. *Everything You Need to Know for a Cassette Ministry: Cassettes in the Context of a Total Christian Communication Program*. Minneapolis: Bethany.

———. 1993 *Media in Church and Mission: Communicating the Gospel*. Pasadena, CA: William Carey Library.

———. 1996 *Research in Church and Mission*. Pasadena, CA: William Carey Library.

Stryker, S. 1980. *Symbolic Interactionism: A Social Structural Version*. Menlo Park, CA: Benjamin/Cummings Pub. Co.

Wallman, S. 1983. "Identity Options." In *Minorities: Community and Identity*, edited by C. Fried. New York: Dahlem Konferenzen.

Wasserman, S., and K. Faust. 2016. *Social Network Analysis: Methods and Applications*. Reprint ed. New York: Cambridge University Press.

Westerlung-Cook, S. 2013. "Intercountry Adoption: Color-b(l)Inding the Issues." In *Multiple Identities: Migrants, Ethnicity, and Membership*, edited by P. Spickard, 182–83. Bloomington, IN: Indiana University Press.

Winter, R. 1999. "Going Far Enough: Taking Some Tips from the Historical Record." In *Perspectives on the World Christian Movement: A Reader*, edited by Ralph D. Winter and Steven C. Hawthorn. Pasadena, CA: William Carey Library.

Woodberry, J. D., and R. G. Shubin. 2001. "Muslims Tell 'Why I Chose Jesus,'" *Mission Frontiers* (March): 28–33.

5 CONFRONTING GOSPEL BARRIERS
Harley Talman

Obliteration or Negotiation?

Introduction

Four decades ago, the Iranian Revolution brought Islam to America's attention. Motivated to better understand this religion that had been thrust into the limelight, I enrolled in a seminary course on Islam. While researching a term paper, I came across Phil Parshall's *The Fortress and the Fire*. That and his subsequent *New Paths in Muslim Evangelism* were significant influences in my thinking about ministry among Muslims. Phil understood that missionaries' actions could either positively or negatively impact people's openness to the gospel. His thinking was so seminal that I have continued to draw from the *New Paths* revised edition in my classes. Phil pioneered new paths that many others have followed or extended in different directions—at times to his delight, and at times to his discomfort. Nonetheless, good fruit has been found among all of them.

Continuing in the path that Phil pioneered, in this chapter I will identify three factors that appear to circumvent increased openness to the gospel among communities affiliated with the major religious traditions. I will focus on the ways in which these factors hinder these people from coming to Christ. These factors arise from a case study in which I was personally involved, and are informed by four decades of ministry experience, as well as my study of mission history. These factors are: (1) cultural differences; (2) religious identity; and (3) communal decision dynamics. In this case study these obstacles were surmounted by God's grace; yet surmounting them required an alternative approach to traditional mission thinking and practice. This alternative approach opened up even more "new paths in Muslim evangelism" and discipleship to Christ.

A Case Study

Some years ago, in a region I will call "Nafa," a violent conflict among ethnic Muslim populations caused a large-scale humanitarian crisis. Atrocities occurred and massive numbers of people were directly or indirectly killed from attacks on civilian populations. This displaced a third of the population. Already living at a subsistence level, they now were in desperate need for food, water, medicine, education, and hope. Many Western humanitarian agencies stepped in and provided emergency relief to the displaced.

I joined an international team, drawn from various agencies, who sought to share God's love through quality humanitarian work with the many Muslim ethnic groups in Nafa. Many of the affected lamented their terrible circumstances; yet one group stood out. They indicated that they had a greater problem: "The sack of sins we carry on our backs!"

Christians working with them offered to show them the Jesus Film. During the viewing of the film, a few objected; but the majority shouted them down, as they wanted to see it. Despite this incredible openness to the gospel, the aid workers were unable to take full advantage of this open door because providing humanitarian aid was overwhelming. Hence, the director began a search for someone who could speak Arabic and focus on evangelism and discipleship.

When we learned of this need, our family responded to the appeal. We were told that because of the violence inflicted by other Muslims, the victims were ready to forsake Islam and become Christians. Crises can lead to increased receptivity to the gospel. Although I was excited for this potential opening for the gospel, my many years of experience among Muslims made me leery about expecting a widespread readiness to convert to Christianity. I recalled Greg Livingstone (the founder of Frontiers) stating that the idea of changing religions for the average Muslim was about as thinkable as the idea of undergoing a sex change operation!

The people of this region spoke many languages, and each ethnic group had strong tribal loyalties. The members of the dominant ethnic group in our area were known throughout the country for their zealous devotion to their conservative values and religious identity. It later became apparent that these factors undergirded their resistance to conversion. I have categorized these three factors as cultural barriers, religious identity, and communal barriers. I will explain how each barrier was surmounted.

Negotiating Cultural Barriers through Incarnational Service and Witness

Many of our aid workers were medical personnel working in health clinics in the camps. Others provided water, food, and supplies. Due to the presence of government authorities, there was little opportunity for any meaningful gospel witness. Officials begrudged and obstructed our relief work because the government itself had been active in instigating indiscriminate military attacks that led to the humanitarian crisis. Therefore, we provided community development work in affected regions outside of the control of the hostile authorities.

One of the projects we undertook was two weeks of training in community health for forty educated men from the villages of one of the war-ravaged areas. During a break, I asked one of the participants (who had previously responded positively to a gospel discussion) if he thought some others would be interested in gathering on our day off to learn about the "other holy books" that Muslims are supposed to believe in.

When I followed up with him a couple of days later, he replied, "Yes." "How many?" I asked. He replied, "They *all* want to come!" Here was a clear case of a crisis increasing receptivity.

In preparing for this meeting, I thought hard about what message would be most appropriate for this group. I had learned early in my ministry to Muslims that traditional Western gospel presentations like the "Four Spiritual Laws" were largely ineffective.[1] I became committed to incarnational communication, which means that the messenger, message, manner, and method must be adapted to and be appropriate for the culture and context. My approach to incarnational communication with the people and context was guided by the following principles:

1. *Begin with, and build on, common ground.* Avoid differences and controversy at the outset.

2. *Employ the terms and vocabulary used in their own language.* Incarnational communication requires speaking the language of the people. Since they are Muslims, their language is going to be "Islamic," with their own religious vocabulary and idioms. These differ from that of the Christian speakers of the same language in that country.

3. *Use the Qur'an as a bridge.* Many Christians refuse to draw from the Qur'an, thinking that to do validates all it teaches. However, apostolic practice

---

1 A typical Muslim response to propositional approaches oriented to addressing the guilt theme is well represented in Hayes, "The Good News for Honor-based Cultures."

justifies appropriating indigenous sources for gospel witness. Paul quoted from pagan poets and prophets in Acts 17; and the New Testament cites noncanonical sources dozens of times.[2]

4. *Preach a "simple" message.* Having taught graduate-level students for years in an Arab seminary, I knew that I needed to replace abstract theological concepts with more practical and relational ones. Thus, utilizing biblical narratives was more appropriate than employing the propositional logic of epistolary literature. In addition, my structuring of thought needed to be simplified. We discovered that some of the village chiefs who had little formal education were not tracking with some of my teaching. I thought that this was due to my dialect, pronunciation, or vocabulary. However, we discovered that their difficulty was in understanding the longer and more complex sentences that I used. Brevity and repetition were keys to learning.

5. *Tell Bible stories.* Discussion of religious doctrines and practices often leads to endless controversy. A chronological Bible storying approach can circumvent many such conflicts. In addition, telling stories of the prophets lays the foundation for presenting Jesus the Messiah as the fulfillment of prophecy and the one chosen by God to establish his kingdom on earth.

6. *Address felt needs.* In selecting stories from the life of Christ, we chose stories that had clear and immediate relevance to their felt needs: e.g., the deliverance of the Gerasene demoniac spoke to their fear and bondage to demonic spirits (Mark 5); the healing of the paralyzed man who was lowered through a roof demonstrated the authority of Jesus both to bring about incredible physical miracle and to forgive sin (Mark 2).

Building bridges, adopting Islamic language, referencing and citing the Qur'an, and telling fascinating stories of the prophets and Jesus enabled us to bypass many obstacles to accurate understanding and acceptance of biblical teaching.

In my experience most cross-cultural Christian workers are willing to adapt to many cultural differences in Islamic contexts, the big exception being the use of their religious terminology, idioms, and texts. Yet, these seemed to have played an important role in giving me credibility and status in what I taught—so much so that my colleagues discovered that the Muslims in their villages were referring to me as *mawlana* ("our sovereign"), a title of highest respect and authority.

---

2 Burer et al., *New Testament,* 802–8; appendix 2: "New Testament Quotations from Outside the Old Testament" has seven pages of verses that reference noncanonical writings. Biblical support for these first three principles may be found in Flemming, *Contextualization in the New Testament,* e.g., his examination in chapter 2 of Paul's three sermons in Acts 2.

Negotiating the Religious Identity Barrier through the Kingdom of God

While incarnational witness and service can overcome cultural barriers, we faced a second, even stronger, source of resistance to conversion—that of religious identity.

This was confirmed when the health workers gathered with us to learn about the "other" holy books. We asked their sheikh to ask Allah's blessing on our time, which then was followed by the prayer of one of my national Christian colleagues. I had only been speaking for a short time when their religious leader interrupted to ask if he could have the floor and address the group. My inner reaction was, "Oh, no! He's going to tell them, 'You can listen if you like, but just remember, we don't believe all of this—we're Muslims!'"

I asked him to wait until I finished the story, and inwardly I hoped that I could keep on going. But after a few minutes he raised his hand again, requesting to address the group. I finally yielded, moved to the back of the room, and sat down next to my colleague. The sheikh addressed the group in their tribal language, which I did not know—so I asked my colleague to translate for me. To my surprise, the sheikh was endorsing my teaching and strongly encouraged them to pay attention to it. He repeatedly expressed gratitude for my teaching them.

He went on and on, so I asked my colleague why the sheikh was doing this. He said, "With this new teaching, people are getting uncomfortable and nervous, because they think you are going to ask them to change their religion." Their sheikh was trying to reassure them otherwise, emphasizing that it was important and good for them as Muslims to hear these stories. After ten minutes or so, he asked me to resume. Providence had provided us with a "man of peace."

A national Christian later confirmed the strength of this resistance. He told me that if our humanitarian aid agency had come to this region before the conflict erupted, the people would have thrown stones at our vehicles! We came to understand that their motivation in coming to our teaching session on the other holy books was not because of a disaffection with Islam. Rather, it was because they were curious about us: We were not like the "Christians" (secularized Westerners) in the other aid agencies—we were good *kafirs* (infidels)! They were interested to learn about us and our beliefs, but they had zero (or rather negative) interest in converting to another religion. The fact that the government's military forces who were trying to destroy them were Muslims was not a source of disillusionment with Islam for them—the problem was that their enemies were *bad* Muslims!

This incident alerted us to how strong their ties to their Islamic identity were. Thereafter when we met with other groups to present the Scriptures, my national coworker decided to meet the issue head-on from the outset. When we met with the next group, after the invocation he began the first session by asking, "What are the blessings of ignorance?" Discussion was very brief—ignorance does not breed blessings. He then explained that we were going to give them some new information, and that knowledge is a good thing. But what they decided to do with this information was completely up to them—i.e., trying to get them to change their religion was not our agenda. They could relax.

In introducing the message of the previous Scriptures—the *Tawrat, Zabur* and *Injil* (Torah, Psalms, and Gospels)—I explained that the purpose of these books was not to establish or promote a religion; rather, they tell the story of the kingdom of God.[3] This established common ground, since Muslims also believe in the kingdom of God. The Qur'an uses the phrase but four times, and with little elaboration. Thus, most Muslims do not know much about it. This uncluttered common ground provided opportunity to build upon it with biblical content. I began by telling the story of Creation, in which the mediatorial aspect of God's rule on earth can be seen. God created Adam as his vice-regent to rule over the creation, his kingdom (Gen 1:28). Adam, the first prophet in Islam,[4] sinned and was removed from the Garden. I told stories of subsequent prophets.

I stated that each prophet had two functions: (1) to deliver God's message to his generation or the people to whom he was sent, and (2) to point the way back to God. Most prophets also provided a sign that pointed to the one who in the future would return us to God and establish his kingdom. I wrote in a diagram the name of each prophet about whom I told a story, and drew an arrow pointing forward to the future. I then explained how each prophet was a road sign marking the way to God's kingdom.

I asserted that the prophets represent the best of human beings and examples for us to emulate. But even so, they were not able to return us to paradise, because they too were sinners. Though contrary to the common Islamic belief that prophets are protected from sin, I supported my assertion with a famous hadith: "Every son of Adam is a sinner, and the best of sinners are those who repent."[5]

---

3 For a presentation of the biblical case for this paradigm, see Taylor, "The Kingdom of God."

4 Though Adam is never called a prophet or messenger in the Qur'an, Islamic tradition (like parts of Jewish tradition) regards him as one.

5 This can be found in books of hadith, available at Islamic websites like www.sunnah.com: https://sunnah.com/urn/2054390.

God eventually established his kingdom rule through the nation of Israel. But the nation likewise failed in its responsibility. Nevertheless, the prophets predicted the kingdom's future establishment through a king of God's choosing—the anointed one, the Messiah. Finally, there came the prophet *Yahya* (John the Baptist), who announced that the kingdom was imminent and that it was to be initiated by Jesus, son of Mary, God's designated king.

I explained that Jesus alone qualified for this mission. Because of his virgin birth, Jesus was not a son of Adam, but the son of Mary, the pure Word of God become flesh. Therefore, he is the only prophet who was sinless and able to return us to paradise. Establishing the kingdom of God was the mission of Jesus (Matt 4) and the theme of his teaching (Matt 5–7) and of those who came after him. The prophets pointed to the way; but Jesus declared, "I am the way" (John 14:6) that the prophets were pointing to.

Without specifying names, I stated that other messengers (apostles) and prophets came after Jesus. I drew arrows pointing *back* to him and quoted the Scripture verse: "All the prophets testify about him that everyone who believes in him receives forgiveness of sins through his name" (Acts 10:43 NIV). (Christians will think of New Testament prophets or those with the charismatic gift of prophecy, while Muslims think of Muhammad. But the most important thing is that if they are prophets from God, their role is to point people to the Way, *'Isa al-Masih*).

The stories and teaching were enthusiastically received, and the health workers asked if we could continue the following week. We did so and had another great time—they loved the stories of the prophets (culminating with Jesus). Afterward we offered them printed copies of the New Testament (*Injil*), as well as audio recordings. They received them most gladly and returned to their villages with much joy.

A few weeks later, we conducted management training for more than thirty village chiefs (*sheiks*). They too were interested in gathering on their day off to learn about the other holy books. Once again, I taught stories of the prophets from "Genesis to Jesus." We then took a short break. After teaching at length in the heat in a foreign language, I was exhausted. I wanted to turn over the teaching to my national colleague. But he groaned, "I'm so sick I can't even stand up. You have to teach!"

I was dazed and at a loss as to what to do. My wife had been sitting in the back of the room, listening to my teaching and observing the audience's response. She interjected, "You have been teaching about the kingdom of God. Why don't you give them an opportunity to enter?" I assumed that many more sessions of teaching would be required before they would be willing to take such a step. For want of a better idea, I agreed.

When we resumed, I reviewed the stories that I had taught and asked them if they understood everything? They replied in the affirmative. Then I asked if they believed everything that I had taught. They replied, "Yes … except the part about Jesus dying on the cross." "Why not?" I asked them (already knowing the answer). The Islamic objection to the crucifixion of Christ is based on a superficial reading of surah 4:157, which refutes the Jews' claim that they crucified and killed the Messiah Jesus, son of Mary. I pointed out that this verse does not deny that Jesus died; rather it only rejects the Jewish claim that *they* killed him. I then quoted other Quranic verses on the issue, two of which indicate (quite clearly in Arabic, unlike most translations into other languages) that God was the one who caused Jesus to die. Then I declared, "The Qur'an says that the Jews didn't kill Jesus. If they didn't do it, then who did? With smiling faces they shouted out in unison, "Allah did!" and broke out in applause! I was astonished, but they were obviously delighted that what I had been teaching was consistent with what the Qur'an taught (though contrary to the common teaching of the clerics).

I then drew a diagram called "the Kingdom Circles"[6] and explained that four of its aspects are characteristic of any kingdom. First, is its location. The kingdom of God exists where God's will is done, where people are submitted to him. Our Master Jesus indicated this in his teaching us to pray: "Your kingdom come, your will be done, on earth as it is in heaven" (Matt 6:10). Second, there are citizens in a kingdom. The Beatitudes (Matt 5:3–11) characterize the citizens in God's kingdom (the poor in spirit, merciful, meek, peacemakers, etc.). Third, is the constitution or law of the kingdom of God. This was Jesus' teaching, summarized in the Sermon on the Mount (Matt 5–7). Fourth, there must be a king. God is king, but he rules through his representative, his "anointed one," the Messiah, 'Isa al-Masih.

I then described the different ways that they could enter the kingdom. I told them that it was up to them to decide how they wanted to enter: (1) They could enter from where they were as Muslims, or (2) they could become Christians and enter the kingdom as we had, or (3) if they liked, they could even enter the kingdom by becoming Jews—they laughed hysterically at the third option!

I then explained that if they believed that Jesus was God's chosen king, the one through whom God provided salvation and forgiveness, and if they were willing to follow him, then they could enter the kingdom. Then I said, "If this is your decision, then raise your hand." *All* of them raised their hands!

My initial reaction was not elation, but disappointment—obviously they had not understood me! So, I began to explain again. But they quickly

---

6 For the origins of this tool, see Bishop, *Boundless*, 121–24.

interrupted, "No! We understand. We want to follow *'Isa!*" I could scarcely believe it. Was this too good to be true? While theoretically possible, on a practical and experiential level, it was difficult for me to imagine that every last person in the group had decided to follow Christ. This brings us to a third barrier: the phenomenon of group decision-making.

Negotiating the Communal Barrier through Group Decision-Making

We might naturally wonder whether each and every individual in the aforementioned group clearly understood the gospel and decided to follow Christ. Did some see others' hands go up and just follow the crowd? This unfamiliar phenomenon raises even more questions. What is meant by "group decisions"? What are their causes and dynamics? Are they soteriologically valid?

Group Decisions in Mission History and Scripture

The highly respected scholar of mission history, Andrew Walls, asserts that making disciples can encompass an entire people group or community, not just individuals: "Conversion to Christ does not isolate the convert from his or her community."[7] Moreover, Kenneth Scott Latourette, the great historian of Christian mission, asserted:

> More and more we must dream in terms of winning groups, not merely individuals. Too often, with our Protestant, nineteenth century individualism, we have torn men and women, one by one, out of the family, village or clan, with the result that they have been permanently de-racinated and maladjusted… Experience, however, shows that it is much better if an entire natural group—a family, village cast or tribe—can come rapidly over into the faith.[8]

Regrettably, workers from the West frequently overlook this. Our neglect is both astonishing and tragic, given the works of Warneck, Pickett, McGavran, Tippett, Winter, and others. Timothy Tennent observes, "We now have over a century of sustained missiological research, both exegetical and field work, to support the validity of such group conversions."[9]

Based on these studies, as well as those of scholars of mission history, Alex Smith concludes, "From the earliest centuries of the church, family, group and people movements were foundational to the extension of the church."[10] Ironically, many American churches have forgotten the ecclesiastical heritage

---

7   Walls, *The Missionary Movement in Christian History*, 51.
8   Cited in Hibbert "Missionary Facilitation of New Movements to Christ," 189.
9   Tennent, *Theology in the Context of World Christianity*, 99.
10 Smith, "Evangelizing Whole Families."

of their forefathers in northern Europe who became Christian through group movements.[11]

Perhaps the reason we ignore this is because of our culture, experience, and theology. Culturally, a supreme value in Western societies is individual autonomy. The importance of deciding for oneself teaches us to ignore "groupthink." Experientially, our evangelism focuses on individuals, as we call them to respond to the gospel. Typical large evangelistic meetings are comprised of individuals from multiple families and social networks, most of whom are already believers. Therefore, the "altar call" is issued to individual nonbelievers to come forward on their own, for it is an individual's decision.

Our culture and experience, in turn, significantly influence our biblical exegesis and theology, blinding us to the reality of group conversion in the New Testament. Hidden from most Western evangelicals is the group conversion in John 4. The village turned out to interview Jesus and they collectively invited him to spend time with them (John 4:40).

After two days, many told the woman, "We no longer believe just because of what you said; now we have heard for ourselves, and we know that this man really is the Savior of the world" (John 4:42, NIV).

While the entire village did not come to faith, this was nonetheless a group decision.

A further example of the influence of our individualistic perspective regarding decision-making and conversion is evident in our interpretation of Jesus' words in the Great Commission. Most Bible versions translate Matthew 28:19 that Jesus' disciples were to "make disciples *of* (or *from*) all nations." But his actual command, *matheeteúsate pánta tá éthnee*, is literally "to disciple the nations." This corporate discipling of peoples is preserved in several translations.[12]

In addition, the missionary activity of the church includes instances of household conversions: Cornelius, Lydia, the Philippian jailer, Crispus (the synagogue ruler) and Stephanas (Acts 10:24, 44–47; 16:15, 34; 18:8; 1 Cor 1:16). Western interpreters tend to downplay these specific examples of household conversion; yet Lenski regards household conversion as standard apostolic practice.[13]

Tennent asserts that part of our discomfort relates to our focus on the judicial aspect of the atonement, which is more individually focused. He discusses the impact of cultural anthropology on theology—e.g., theories

---

11 McGavran, *The Bridges of God*, 38.
12 Some examples are the King James, Douay-Rheims, Webster, Young's Literal, Jubilee Bible 2000, Aramaic in Plain English, and the Arabic Smith-Van Dyke.
13 Lenski, *The Interpretation of the Acts of the Apostles*, 661

of the atonement—but also their application to the process of conversion. He correctly observes that in most Buddhist, Hindu, and Muslim cultures, which are shame-based, the socio-cultural factors are even greater barriers to the gospel than the theological barriers. Westerners are uncomfortable with the concept of group conversion, because of their conviction that each individual must repent and accept Christ. In contrast, those in collectivist societies think as a group, and it is the entire group that comes to faith or rejects the gospel.[14] Tennent observes,

> In a collective, shame-based culture, it is difficult to act in isolation from others, especially those senior to you. The New Testament writers seem to recognize this reality, and therefore encourage entire households to come together to minimize the social dislocation and avoid the charge that one person has brought shame on the rest of the family. We should remember that the source of the shame is not so much tied to the propositional content of the Christian message as it is to the scandalizing notion that someone may be acting independently from the will of the larger group.[15]

Tennent reassures Westerners that group conversion does not obviate the need for individual faith. Rather, the conversion of a social network should be viewed as a "multicoordinated personal decision," in which large numbers are choosing to follow Jesus in "a single movement" instead of through dozens of isolated decisions, independent of each other[16]—such as the three thousand Jews who believed at Pentecost. In a nutshell, Tennent asserts that "Christian conversion is always personal, but not necessarily individualistic."[17]

McGavran sought to explain the psychology of such societies for whom "individual action is treachery.... Only a rebel would strike out alone, without consultation and without companions. The individual does not think of himself as a self-sufficient unit, but as part of a group."[18] The issues of one's life—e.g., business matters, marriage of children, personal difficulties—entail group thinking and decisions. McGavran clarifies that group decisions are

> the sum of separate individual decisions. The leader makes sure that his followers will follow. The followers make sure that they are not ahead of each other. Husbands sound out wives. Sons pledge their fathers. "Will we as a group move if so-and-so does not come?" is a frequent question.... A change of religion involves a community change. Only as its members move together, does change become healthy and constructive.[19]

---

14 Tennent, *Theology in the Context of World Christianity*, 98.
15 Ibid.
16 Ibid.
17 Ibid., 99.
18 McGavran, *The Bridges of God*, 11.
19 Ibid., 12.

I would add my belief that the amount of understanding in such "personal" decisions may be quite different from those that societies are more "individualistic." In group-oriented societies, members generally accept the decisions of their leaders as their own—in that sense they are "personal" decisions, even if they have little understanding of the basis for the leader's decision. In individualistic societies, much more understanding is required.

Let me offer an example. After years of gospel teaching, Vincent Donovan decided the Masai community was ready for baptism. But he was unwilling to baptize some in various villages who had not attended his classes. The elders insisted, "You either baptize all of us or none of us, for we refuse to be divided."[20] Realizing the force of the communal bonds and that the elders' decisions were accepted by the group, Donovan relented and baptized the communities in their entirety.

McGavran also observed that the motivation or process by which decisions for Christ are made (individual versus group) is not the crucial issue, but rather what happens afterward. What is critical is the effort devoted to what he termed "perfecting" (what most others call "follow-up" and "discipling") of these "disciples" (what others call converts or new believers). If properly taught, those in people movements can become as spiritually mature as those who made well-informed individualistic decisions for Christ.

This is exactly what I observed among the sheikhs who had raised their hands together in deciding to follow Jesus. Many weeks later, Sheikh Adam made the two-hour trip to our clinic to bring the sheikh of a hostile group that had raided his village for treatment. Adam heard that this sheikh had a medical need and had to walk quite a distance to get to him (his donkey having been stolen in an earlier raid by the other sheikh's people). What motivated Adam to help his adversary? None of us had told him to. However, we had taught the sheikhs Jesus' teaching in the Sermon on the Mount. Sheikh Adam seemed to be obeying the Messiah's command to love your enemies.

On another occasion, after Adam's village was destroyed by enemy soldiers, he sought refuge with relatives in another village. When I saw Adam and expressed my sorrow and sympathy, he replied, "Oh, that's okay, Allah will take care of us. But the problem is that they took our supply of Bibles. There are still many villages that have not heard the gospel!"

Such faith, obedience, and passion for the gospel were greater than I could imagine any of the members of my "individually saved" church displaying after such calamity (myself included)!

Nonetheless, aiming for the conversion of an entire community, people group, or even a social network is seldom in our missiological strategy—despite

---

20 Donovan, *Christianity Rediscovered*, 91.

convincing answers to concerns and objections.[21] Western evangelicals (and those who are the product of Western mission efforts) focus their evangelistic efforts on converting isolated individuals, and then forming them into a new community. This is the Western paradigm for church planting. It was mine as well, but the Lord began to change that.

Group Decisions in Our Mission Practice

Our practice had been to teach groups of leaders who had relationships with one another. As we presented biblical stories and interacted with these groups of leaders, we perceived enough receptivity to ask for them to respond, hoping for numerous individual decisions. Our Bible teaching emerged in the context of our working with these groups in community development. Interacting with these same leaders regarding community organization or development projects, we taught and discussed matters until a consensus developed—whereby they could make a group decision about what the community should do.

Ironically, when presenting the gospel with our Western individualistic mindset, we could only envision numbers of "individual decisions." When all of the sheikhs raised their hands together to signal their desire to follow Christ, I was confronted with a new phenomenon—different dynamics were operating. Thus, the Lord began guiding us to seek to facilitate a consensus among the leaders, leading a group decision about the gospel. The process by which a group decision would be reached was not something I had planned out.

During a subsequent development training in another region, more than seventy village sheikhs participated. At the end of each day, we taught them the same Scripture stories that we had previous groups. Following each story, the leaders would ask questions and discuss the issues with us and one another.

After the third day, we reached a point at which previous groups had responded to the gospel, and I was about to call for a decision. But before I did, I was startled as these words entered my mind: "What are you doing? Do you need to have them raise their hands as a response to know that I'm at work: So you can feel like I am using you? So you can give a report that will impress your supporters?" I silently replied, "No, Lord," and sat down.

My colleague continued teaching Bible stories. By the end of the next day, I noticed that the most influential leaders were expressing positive comments about our teaching; those who had previously disputed issues or expressed negative responses were now silent. It dawned on me: "They have decided— they have embraced the gospel message!" But my American democratic convictions protested: "How can they decide like that—they didn't even take

---

21 In "Evangelizing Whole Families," Smith effectively rebuts the typical objections to this strategy as well as offers practical steps in winning entire families to Christ.

a vote!" I came to realize that decision-making dynamics in group-oriented societies may differ from ours, but they are a natural process for them. At our graduation ceremony at the end of the week, they thanked us for the community-development training—but most of all, for the spiritual training in God's Word.

Weeks later, my national coworkers returned to that area, and the community gathered with them. During the previous visit, one of the stories we taught them was the story of Creation. Now one of the local men informed our team that he had composed a song about that story. Using a local musical genre, he sang out what God had created on each day, and the group sang a response. My colleagues then taught them a new story, and after discussing it, they concluded with prayer. Upon our return, one team member told me, "I think we've just been to church" (singing, Scripture reading, prayer, and fellowship in the gathered community). We didn't need to bring individual believers together and create a new structure—a church. Rather, we brought the gospel into the already existing social network—and the community became the church.

Conclusion

In the case study in this chapter, an opportunity for gospel advance was hindered by three obstacles: cultural, religious, and communal barriers. Each one was surmounted: (1) the cultural barrier through incarnational witness and service; (2) the religious identity barrier through the message of the kingdom of God (versus the religion of Christianity); and (3) the communal barrier through group consensus decisions for Christ.

Historically, the lion's share of gospel advance has been among the minor religious traditions (animists, polytheists, local and tribal deities). Until recently the major non-Christian religious traditions (Buddhist, Hindu, Sikh, Muslim, Jewish, etc.) have been the least impacted, due to the cultural, religious identity, and communal barriers discussed in this chapter.

While the missiological approach followed in the case study should not be viewed as a "silver bullet" or automatic formula for success, mission leaders and practitioners should give it serious missiological reflection. The concepts of incarnational communication, entering the kingdom of God (versus adopting a new religion) as a paradigm for mission, and group conversions are not completely unknown to missiology. However, they are the "road less traveled" in Western evangelical missions.

We need to reflect on the reasons for our reticence. Are they due to ignorance? Or the discomfort with diverging from our ecclesiastical tradition or missiological methods? Or fear of controversy? Or personal difficulty in adopting incarnational communication and service? Or are they due to theological constraints? If no other purpose is served, may this chapter encourage exploration and discussion of these issues, leading to applications that more effectively prepare gospel workers.

Phil Parshall pioneered "new paths in Muslim evangelism" for his generation. May his "tribe" increase as heirs of his missiology surmount the cultural, religious identity, and communal barriers in order to extend the kingdom of God to all peoples of the planet!

References

Bishop, B. 2015. *Boundless: What Global Expressions of Faith Teach Us About Following Jesus.* Grand Rapids, MI: Baker.

Burer, Michael H., W. Hall Harris, Daniel B. Wallace, Eberhard and Erwin Nestle, Kurt and Barbara Aland. 2004. *New Testament: New English Translation, Novum Testamentum Graece.* Dallas: NET Bible Press.

Donovan, V. 2003. *Christianity Rediscovered.* Maryknoll, NY: Orbis.

Flemming, D. 2005. *Contextualization in the New Testament: Patterns for Theology and Mission.* Downers Grove, IL: InterVarsity Press.

Hayes, J. 2015. "The Good News for Honor-based Cultures." *Mission Frontiers* 37:1 (Jan–Feb): 29–31.

Hibbert, R. 2012. "Missionary Facilitation of New Movements to Christ." *International Journal of Frontier Missiology* 29:4 (Winter): 189–95.

Lenski, R. C. H. 1964. *The Interpretation of the Acts of the Apostles.* Minneapolis, MN: Augsburg.

McGavran, D. A. 1955. *The Bridges of God.* New York: Friendship Press.

_____. 1980. *Understanding Church Growth*, rev. ed. Grand Rapids, MI: Eerdmans.

Parshall, P. 1975. *The Fortress and the Fire: Jesus Christ and the Challenge of Islam.* Bombay: Gospel Literature Service.

_____. 1980. *New Paths in Muslim Evangelism.* Grand Rapids: Baker Book House.

_____. 2003. *Muslim Evangelism: Contemporary Approaches to Contextualization.* Waynesboro, GA: Gabriel Publishing. Revised edition of *New Paths in Muslim Evangelism.*

Smith, A. G. 2012. "Evangelizing Whole Families: The Value of Families in the 21st Century." *Mission Frontiers*, March–April.

Taylor, A. 2015. "The Kingdom of God: A biblical paradigm for mission." In *Understanding Insider Movements: Disciples of Jesus within Diverse Religious Communities*, edited by H. Talman and J. Travis, 173–80.

Tennent, T. 2007. *Theology in the Context of World Christianity: How the Global Church Is Influencing the Way We Think about and Discuss Theology.* Grand Rapids, MI: Zondervan.

Walls, A. 1996. *The Missionary Movement in Christian History: Studies in the Transmission of Faith.* Maryknoll, NY: Orbis.

6 Two Decades of the Letter "C"

Joseph S. Williams

Reflections on the C1-C6 Spectrum

In 1997, I made my first foray into missions as a recent college graduate. I went to a post-Soviet, Muslim-majority country in Central Asia with the intent of exploring my calling to the Muslim world. During my two years there, unbeknownst to me two articles were published in *Evangelical Missions Quarterly* that would both trouble and inform my years of service in Muslim Central Asia. When I returned to the US in 1999 and was pursuing a seminary degree, I read those two articles as part of my training. One was John Travis's "C1 to C6 Spectrum."[1] The other was Phil Parshall's provocatively titled response: "Danger! New Directions in Contextualization."[2] For those at my seminary and church who were interested in missions, the "C" issue was front and center. We were all ready to define ourselves by the letter "C," along with an appropriate number from 1 to 6.

I write now after more than fifteen years of living and working among Muslims in two countries in Central Asia. I no longer wish to define myself by the letter "C" and a number. I do, however, find the foundational questions of a debate made public by those initial articles to be of ongoing concern to the task of missions among Muslims. In this chapter, in honor of Phil Parshall's tremendous contributions to the issues of contextualization and mission among Muslims, I will lay out my own series of "Cs" both in summary of the debate raised by those two seminal articles and in anticipation of their ongoing impact. The five C's I will address are Controversies, Clarifications, Challenges, Continuation, and Cautions.

---

1 Travis, "The C1 to C6 Spectrum."
2 Parshall, "Danger! New Directions in Contextualization."

Controversies

In this section, I will first outline the basic elements of the spectrum and summarize Parshall's response to the model. Then I will mention important clarifications that have emerged since Parshall and Travis's 1998 articles. Travis listed six ways that groups of believers in Jesus from Muslim backgrounds, at the time, were expressing their faith in Christ in terms of language, culture, and religious identity. Travis called this the spectrum of "Christ-centered communities," hence the "C-Spectrum."[3] The spectrum has often been read as a "contextualization" scale, and that is how I read it in 2000. C1 meant far from local culture and C5 or C6 meant the gospel could be indistinguishable from local culture.

Note that the intended "C" of the spectrum is closer in meaning to "church" than "contextualization."[4] Travis's "C-Spectrum" was about existing "churches" within a Muslim context. These "Christ-centered communities" all work out how to "retain," "reinterpret," and "reject" elements of their own culture in relationship to foreign cultures as they live out devotion to Jesus as Savior.[5] These communities are highly varied, just as they vary in their location around the globe.

The spectrum itself presented three main areas of distinction between the different ways *gathered* believers from Muslim backgrounds "worship Jesus as Lord":[6] language, culture, and religious identity. Each number on the scale indicates a different aspect of these three dimensions that is different from the one to the left. To show these different aspects, below I have indicated the key difference from one number to the next. For instance, the difference between C1 and C2 hinges on which language is used in the gathered community of believers. The chart on the following page is how I have visualized the spectrum.

Parshall's focus, however, was on "contextualization," as his own article's title indicated.[7] Contextualization has tended to mean the work that a "foreign missionary" does to explain the gospel and its implications in context.[8] Parshall's own work[9] describes potentially controversial ideas that moved missionaries deeper into the practice, thought, and community of Muslims to whom they sought to explain the gospel. In *Muslim Evangelism*, for instance, Parshall opens up questions about baptism, prostrations,

3 The original article was defined as a "spectrum," but it is often called a "scale." I have retained the original term in this article.

4 I have confirmed this in personal correspondence with Travis.

5 See Travis and Travis, Travis and Travis, "Roles of 'Alongsiders' in Insider Movements," 162. In the original article (1998), Travis only mentions "reject" and "reinterpret."

6 Travis, "The C1–C6 Spectrum After Fifteen Years: Misunderstandings, Limitations, and Recommendations," 492.

7 Parshall, "Danger! New Directions in Contextualization."

8 Contextualization may not be explicitly defined this way, but in Parshall's own writings it clearly comes out as the framework for the discussion.

9 See Parshall, *Muslim Evangelism: Contemporary Approaches to Contextualization*. The original edition was Parshall, *New Paths in Muslim Evangelism: Evangelical Approaches to Contextualization*.

The "C-Spectrum"

Christ-centered communities among Muslims and how they relate to language, culture, and identity

Category	C1	C2	C3	C4	C5	C6
Language	Non-native	Native	Native	Native	Native	C1-C5
Culture	Non-native	Non-native	Religiously "neutral."* Local culture retained.	Retain many religious forms but give them fresh biblical meaning.	Retain many religious forms but give them fresh biblical meaning.	C1-C5
Religious Identity	"Christian"	"Christian"	"Christian"	"Jesus Follower." "Usually not seen as Muslims by the Muslim community."***	"Legally and socially within the community of Islam."**	C1-C5

* Travis, "The C1 to C6 Spectrum: A Practical Tool."

** Ibid.

*** Ibid. Additionally, Travis argues that C5 believers "Meet regularly with other C5 believers" and "Unsaved Muslims may see C5 believers as theologically deviant and may eventually expel them from the community of Islam."

liturgy, holidays, etc. The framework for these questions is often the missionary's position on these issues and the missionary's promotion of them.

Parshall's response to the C Spectrum in 1998 focused particularly on the role of the missionary. His primary critique in "Danger! New Directions in Contextualization" was the possibility of foreign missionaries identifying as Muslims—a point that never comes up in Travis's C-Spectrum. But Parshall was also concerned that the pursuit of C5 models would lead to sub-biblical theological communities. He cites a study on a community of believers who identified as Muslims, confessed Jesus as their only Savior, but had mixed views on the Trinity and the role of the Qur'an.

In a sense, then, the debate of the past two decades has essentially been two debates, sometimes overlapping and sometimes occupying separate domains of concern. On the one hand, the question is how missiologists view, describe, and engage existing and burgeoning movements to Christ with a variety of expressions and ways of relating to MBBs' birth cultures. On the other hand, the question is how foreign missionaries themselves should engage Muslims with the gospel and the role they should play in discipling believers within the context of the missionaries' host cultures.

The tension between these two questions has much to do with whether the spectrum is prescriptive or descriptive. The heat of the debate, in one sense, has been over the degree to which any of the spots is the target for discipleship. Though there are critics of C4,[10] the primary conflict has been between the C4 and C5 regions of the spectrum. The distinction between the two, in Travis's original C-Spectrum, was that the C4 communities defined themselves as outside the "religious"[11] identity of their birth community, whereas the C5 communities tended toward retaining their formal or "legal"[12] religious identity within their birth community.

Travis did not explain how Muslim background believers might continue to relate to the mosque, the *Shahada* (Islamic creed) and the Qur'an. Rather, he simply noted that they retain a "Muslim" identity in their community, even as they deviate theologically from their birth community, particularly regarding Jesus' death, resurrection, and personhood, and the reliability and importance of the Old and New Testaments. The unaddressed questions in Travis's brief article, as evidenced

---

10 Dixon, "When C4 Is Not Biblical in Many Respects."
11 I use quotation marks in the first use of this term "religious," for reasons that I will explain in a later section, but I will refrain from doing so in future instances. Yet it should be clear that this is one of the disputed terms in this discussion.
12 Travis, "The C1 to C6 Spectrum."

in Parshall's response, became a prime concern for those debating and applying the spectrum regarding its application to Muslim evangelism.[13]

As I have engaged the C Spectrum over the past two decades and considered its future use, I have sought to parse out the different descriptive elements and prescriptive interpretations of it. Next, I will address both descriptive and prescriptive approaches, particularly as they relate to my engagement with the spectrum on the field.

Clarifications

In my own pre-field reckoning with the C Spectrum, I had misconceptions about the C5 category that had to be clarified both through a better understanding of the terms being used and through face-to-face interactions with believers who could be considered C5. I have found that many missiologists and practitioners shared these misconceptions. This lack of clarity often distracted from meaningful discussion about missionary strategies. In this section, I seek to remove those obstacles and get to the core issues involved for both the descriptive and prescriptive tasks on the field. In particular, I have identified three key clarifications missiologists need to make regarding the C5 category.

First, many have posited that C5 communities simply seek to avoid persecution.[14] This has been consistently denied by observers of C5 communities. As Higgins, Jameson, and Travis note in their article, "Misunderstandings about Insider Movements," C5 believers are persecuted. C5 believers have been killed, imprisoned, tortured, and harassed for their allegiance to Jesus.[15] Some of the C5 believers I have met on the field have experienced death threats and exile. A proper understanding of the scale recognizes that C6 believers (by definition) are in the difficult position of hiding their faith for fear of persecution. The C6 category could be understood as a secret expression of any of the C1-C5 categories.[16]

---

13 Many of the articles have been collated into a couple volumes. Additionally, Corwin's exchange with C5 observers in 2007 provided a substantive description for the discussion. See Corwin, "A Humble Appeal to C5/Insider Movement Muslim Ministry Advocates to Consider Ten Questions." See also Talman and Travis, eds., *Understanding Insider Movements: Disciples of Jesus Within Diverse Religious Communities*; and Lingel, Morton, and Nikkedes, eds., *Chrislam: How Missionaries Are Promoting an Islamized Gospel*.

14 See Ayub, "Observations and Reactions to Christians Involved in a New Approach to Mission"; and Morse, "Why Are So Many So Silent? The Insider Movement in America."

15 Higgins cites a specific C5 leader who was "repeatedly beaten, given electric shocks, hung upside down by his feet … and forced to watch several men have their throats cut." Higgins, Jameson, and Talman, "Myths and Misunderstandings About Insider Movements," Location 1680.

16 According to my correspondence with John and Ann Travis, this was not their intention. Because C1-C5 are defined as groups, an individual hidden believer does not fit into any of those categories. I work in a setting with few gathered groups and have tended to see the spectrum in light of identity, language, and culture for both individuals and groups. In this sense, I am speaking of the secret believer's disposition toward those five categories.

Relatedly, the second clarification is in regard to the misconception that the retention of one's religious identity from birth, particularly the term "Muslim," involves no change in allegiance or theological formulation. In particular, we tend to rigidly associate the identity term "Muslim" with traditional Islamic positions that oppose central biblical teachings, like Jesus' divinity and crucifixion.[17] This assumption misunderstands the spectrum and the terms of description. C5 believers, though retaining a nominal affiliation with their birth community and social connectedness, have reoriented their theology and lives toward Jesus as Lord and Savior. This is a radical departure in conviction from the faith of their birth communities. Some have proposed that this dynamic is best explained as "cultural insider/theological outsider." Over the past fifteen years, I have met C3, C4, and C5 believers on the field. Each kind of believer has a dramatic account of conversion tied to Jesus' transformative power.

This leads to a final clarification from the spectrum's original definition, namely, that C5 believers have no expression of "church" as a distinguishing community of believers. Tennent infers, for instance, that the C5 approach is primarily individualistic without any corporate gatherings.[18] And Nikides argues that C5 believers do not baptize or practice the Lord's Supper.[19] Yet the statements at the beginning of this chapter showed that the *gathering of believers* was crucial to defining all the Cs of the spectrum. Moreover, Higgins and Naja both describe sacraments as being part of the C5 movements they studied.[20] Insofar as "doing church" refers to multiple believers gathering for prayer, worship, and reading of the Christian Scriptures, the C5 part of the spectrum fits this description.

Challenges

Recognizing the key clarifications regarding elements of the C Spectrum, I have observed ongoing challenges that the C1-C6 Spectrum, and the debate surrounding it, exposes for practitioners like myself: the tension between prescriptive and descriptive approach; the difficulty of distinguishing between religion, culture, and identity; and the evolving definitions of syncretism. I turn to those challenges now.

Prescriptive or Descriptive?

I have already noted the tension within debate surrounding the C Spectrum between prescriptive and descriptive approaches. For myself, I found that I was

---

17 See Dixon, "Moving on From the C1-C6 Spectrum"; Nikides, "A Response to Kevin Higgins' 'Inside What? Church, Religion and Insider Movements in Biblical Perspective'"; and Smith, "An Assessment of the Insider's Principle Paradigms."
18 Tennent, "Followers of Jesus (Isa) in Islamic Mosques.'"
19 Nikides, "A Response," 97–98.
20 Higgins, "Speaking," 67; Naja, "Sixteen Features," 156.

inclined to take the descriptive elements of the C1-6 spectrum and turn them into "ministry targets." As others have done, I idealized the C4 category when I entered the field, believing that space entailed gospel integrity: these groups were not co-opted by foreign identity, but stayed pure in light of the corrupting influences of Islam. I sympathized with Parshall's desire to avoid the risks of syncretism assumed to be part of the C5 space.

Yet I have found that simply using the C1-C6 spectrum to prescribe a certain plot on the continuum oversimplifies the task of missions in the Muslim context in two significant ways. First, the spectrum, as all heuristic tools must do, assumes distinctions that can be extremely difficult to tease out in real life— namely the distinction between religion and culture. Second, and relatedly, the problem of "syncretism" and its place on the spectrum continually tempts us to engage in "arm-chair missiology." In other words, we can too easily be drawn to evaluate and second-guess decisions others make (local believers and missionaries) outside of our own ministry context. These two issues are problematic for our use of the spectrum and application of it and, hence, bring us into the two additional challenges the C1-C6 Spectrum faces.

The Difficulty of Distinguishing between Religion, Culture, and Identity

I first confronted the tension between religion, culture, and identity when I moved to a small conservative town in Central Asia. My wife and I preferred the local clothing to Western garb and spoke the minority dialect, rather than the trade language or English. We were primarily identified as Muslims for these acts, despite not participating in any religious ceremonies associated with the mosque. Our training had taught us that "clothing" and "language" were cultural issues, not religious. It's been evident to us over the years that this simple division of categories is far from the reality.

The distinction between the C3, C4, and C5 categories hinges on the term "religious." C3 believers use "religiously neutral" forms.[21] C4 and C5 believers use "religious forms," but invest them with biblical meaning.[22] C5 believers retain their birth "religious identity." So much of one's reading of the spectrum depends on one's assumption about what is "religious" and what is "cultural." The social sciences have often demonstrated how "religion" can be a political and social marker as much or more than a theological one.[23]

---

21 Travis, "The C1 to C6 Spectrum."
22 Ibid.
23 See Barth, "Introduction"; Barth, "Enduring and Emerging Issues in the Analysis of Ethnicity." Canfield shows how Barth's paradigm applies to the use of religion as a political marker. See Canfield, *Faction and Conversion in a Plural Society: Religious Alignments in the Hindu Kush.* See also Giuseppe Sciortino, "Ethnicity, Race, Nationhood, Foreignness, and Many Other Things: Prolegomena to a Cultural Sociology of Difference-Based Interactions."

Additionally, it can be difficult to determine what is a "neutral" religious act. For instance, wearing the traditional *shalwar kamees* style of dress for men in which the shirt extends to the man's knees can be understood to be an imitation of the Prophet Mohammad's dress, thus a keeping of the *sunna* (tradition). Was this, then, a statement of loyalty to the Prophet, or merely a cultural decision? In keeping with my experience, anthropologists have long struggled with explaining and defining "religion" as a distinct element of culture.

This particular discussion has a couple of crucial components. On the one hand, there is the question about "essentialism," or definitions of world religion, particularly Islam, that reduce them to their "essential doctrines and practices."[24] Social scientists have increasingly questioned this perspective, suggesting that each community and even each individual engage a variety of practices and beliefs that can hardly be encapsulated under a single umbrella of "Islam."[25]

But communities themselves are often "essentialist" in their definitions of "Muslim." This plays into the repeated concern that C5 believers are deceptive about their core convictions. For instance, if the local community defines "Islam" in one way and C5 believers vary from that depiction theologically, have they not fundamentally left that community? This is a legitimate question. In practice, I have been genuinely surprised at the way different groups and individuals negotiate their identity and practice in order to meet the requirements of Muslim identity in varying circumstances. One friend, for instance, told me about his atheistic convictions while thumbing his prayer beads. I am not commending his convictions. Rather, seeing lines of religious barriers crossed and re-crossed in practice has suggested to me that using "religion" as a primary category within the spectrum has its limitations.

A second component of how difficult it is to distinguish religion, culture, and identity involves ongoing debates about the definition of "religion" and to what degree our current conception of religions and their boundary lines are tied to modernity and the Enlightenment. Brent Nongrbi, in *Before Religion*, argues that common definitions of religion which distinguish it from other elements of society have been "increasingly criticized by experts in various academic fields" over the past thirty years. Historians have "observed that no

24 Daniels, "Conclusion: Learning from the Margins," location 5144.
25 As Marrinci puts it in his *Anthropology of Islam*, "During my years of study, books and teachers explained that Islam is a religion based on theological precepts and a particular history. During my research, I learned that the Islam of books, theology and history is nothing other than a ghost hunted for by both the believers as well as the academics," 472. Yet recognizing the diversity of beliefs and practices still leaves us grappling for words to describe the common elements between these so-called "Islams." As Farah notes on this question, citing Ahmad's *What Is Islam?* there are two errors we can fall into in this discussion: The first error is to place Islam in a rigid framework that is unable to account for the diversity of Muslims around the world who often contradict one another. The second error is to claim that there is no such thing as Islam, but instead only islams imagined by each Muslim. "How Muslims Shape and Use Islam: Towards a Missiological Understanding," location 664.

ancient language has a term that really corresponds to what modern people mean when they say 'religion.'"[26] Moreover, they have discerned that many of the names associated with major religions first emerged after encounters with European Christians.[27] Others note, in this same vein, that the creation and enforcement of religious categories were often associated with Western colonial rule.[28] Increasingly, biblical scholars are alluding to these same issues. N. T. Wright, in his description of the apostle Paul, resists "Post-enlightenment" categories that parse out "religion" as a distinct element of life and culture, seeking in his own work to "put back together the worlds that the Enlightenment split apart."[29]

This is not to say that this perspective on religion and particularly distinct categories of "world religion" is settled. Postcolonial writer Pnina Werbner, for one, maintains there are pre-Enlightenment terms for world religions and the concepts of religion.[30] But the lack of clarity on this issue exposes the tension within the C Spectrum that contributes to the debates surrounding it, let alone its field application.

Evolving Definitions of Syncretism

Another challenge raised by employing the spectrum as a prescriptive model is the nature of syncretism. Parshall's expressed cautions in 1998 concerning the C5 fellowships were that they ran the risk of becoming syncretistic in their ongoing association with the local mosque. Within the C1-6 Spectrum itself, though, where does "syncretism" fit? The short answer is that it doesn't. The spectrum as a descriptive scale simply presents the different ways believers in Muslim contexts are following Jesus. It doesn't detail how successfully they do so.

In practice, I used the spectrum pre-field as a tool to decide what was syncretistic and what was not. As I noted above, I liked the C4 groups instinctively. They seemed to parse out what was good and bad and maintain the purity I idealized. In reality, though, I've found that most groups have syncretistic elements regardless of their approach to culture, language, or identity.

This observation fits with the developing reflections on syncretism over the past forty years. Imbach, for instance, defined syncretism in 1984 in a way that depended on the earlier concept of "essentialist" religion that we noted above. In the Evangelical Dictionary of Theology, he defines it as the "process by which elements of one religion are assimilated into another religion resulting

---

26 Nongbri, *Before Religion*, 7.
27 Ibid.
28 Duerksen and Dyrness, *Seeking Church*; Richard, "Religious Syncretism as a Syncretistic Concept."
29 Wright, *Paul and the Faithfulness of God*, 35.
30 Werbner, "Religious Identity," 238.

in a change in the fundamental tenets or nature of those religions."[31] Imbach's definition raises some of the key questions being asked over the past few decades through this very debate and within the field of anthropology: What is religion? What are the fundamental tenets of a "religion," and to what degree is change bad or unexpected?

This tension is recognized by Moreau in his definition of the term sixteen years later:

> Syncretism. Blending of one idea, practice, or attitude with another. Traditionally among Christians it has been used of the replacement or dilution of the essential truths of the gospel through the incorporation of non-Christian elements.... Syncretism of some form has been seen everywhere the church has existed. We are naïve to think that eliminating the negatives of syncretism is easily accomplished.[32]

Moreau removes the term "religion" from his definition and focuses on the "dilution of essential truths." This moves the discussion toward the issue of convictions; however, they are lived out in the forms of the community, and away from the potential focus on rituals and forms that could dominate Imbach's definition.

Most recently, Shaw[33] and Burrows[34] outline how what may be perceived as "syncretism" can often be part of the necessary process of "hybridity" as the gospel penetrates the core of a community. Shaw, appropriating Hiebert's model of "Critical Contextualization,"[35] describes how even Shamanistic practices among the Samo became redefined in a biblical manner as the tribe redirected "their religious experience toward the creator's intention" in Christ.[36] In the subsequent chapter from the same volume, Burrows describes how our own understanding of this process is in ongoing flux. As he says, "[We] are only beginning to acknowledge the way in which the culture of the evangelizers and the culture of the hearers of the Word interact with one another."[37] He goes on to detail how he understands this process as necessary "hybridity"—not a

---

31 Imbach, ""Syncretism," 1062.
32 Moreau, "Syncretism," 623.
33 Shaw, "The Dynamics of Ritual and Ceremony: Transforming Traditional Rites to Their Intended Purpose."
34 Burrows, "Theological Ideals, Cross-Cultural Realities: Syncretism and Hybridity in Christian Culture Crossings."
35 Hiebert, "Critical Contextualization."
36 In this particular case, Shaw had observed in 1972 the Samo community use glossalalia (tongues) to summon a dead shaman's spirit. Fifteen years later, Shaw discovered (to his great surprise) that after many in the community had come to faith they were speaking in tongues, with interpretation, in their church services, using some of the same musical patterns as the 1972 ritual. This had emerged without the involvement of "Pentecostal" missionaries. Shaw, "Dynamics of Ritual," 14–15.
37 Burrows, "Theological Ideals," 26.

process that dilutes the central message of "God and God's relationship to all of humanity ... in Jesus' ignominious death and logic-defying resurrection," but one that is indeed necessary "when Christian faith begins to mature among a people."[38] From this vantage point, "syncretism" as "hybridity" is "inevitable."[39]

My own encounter with the issue of syncretism led to another crucial development in missiological thinking—namely, that externalism can be as much or more of a cause of syncretism than the mere mixing of ideas. In my early work with believers on the field, I found that external conformity on an issue, including the exclusion of former "religious" activities, did not necessarily mean heart-level engagement with the gospel.

Sometimes in an effort to avoid the mixing of religious categories, missionaries have unintentionally failed to introduce the gospel to the core concerns of a community. This can be quite evident within translation efforts. Harriet Hill describes how the avoidance of theologically loaded local terms actually distorted biblical truth rather than reinforcing it[40]—a point made at length, as well, in Lamen Sanneh's *Translating the Message.*[41]

In short, missiologists have had to reckon with the possibility that hidden presuppositions pose a risk of unbiblical syncretism. Neglecting to dig into the roots of cultural and religious presuppositions leaves them untouched and therefore persistent. This fundamental point has increasingly cautioned me against using the C Spectrum as a "syncretism" diagnostic tool. Each point on the spectrum runs the danger of syncretism, and no point provides an antidote against its dangers.

---

38 Ibid., 27.

39 Ibid.

40 In an effort to avoid using a local term for "demons" that came from the local spiritual language, the translators created a new term for the idea of "demons." As a result, it appears that the local term (and beings) they decided against remained within the believing community's worldview and were largely untouched by the teaching of the Scriptures. Jesus has power to cast out demons (using the new term), but not the supernatural malevolent beings never mentioned in the Scriptures but existing within their previous worldview. This contrasts with what happened when local, non-ideal terms were used. The term for "Satan," though originally implying a sometimes malevolent, sometimes benevolent, being, changed over its eighty years of use in the translated Scriptures. Believers reassigned the meaning of the term to refer to a malevolent being that was opposed to God's will. Hill, "The Effects of Using Local and Non-Local Terms in Mother-Tongue Scripture."

41 The late Catholic missiologist, who came from a Muslim background himself, argued that the use of local terms, even ones linked deeply with existing religions, created a connection with the past necessary for the gospel to engage all elements of the culture. Describing this process in another African language, he writes, "[When] new converts prayed to the God of Jesus Christ as *ndina*, for example, they created an overlap to preserve and perpetuate the earlier notions in the environment of the new dispensation. [This] ... helps to legitimize change and resolve, without bypassing, potential difficulties. The point of convergence remains the familiar medium of the vernacular and its often-hidden presuppositions." Sanneh, *Translating the Message: The Missionary Impact on Culture*, 177.

Continuation

The controversies raised by the C Spectrum are likely to continue, but in the midst of that we do well to learn as much as we can to move forward this discussion in productive and healthy ways. The value of the C Spectrum's continuation, then, depends on our ongoing learning and reflection. For those working in the field—particularly in pioneer settings—what can we make of the issues surrounding the C Spectrum and the challenge it presents on the descriptive and prescriptive fronts?

Regarding the latter, we have tremendous opportunity to keep learning from field developments. In 1998, there were a few movements to Christ among Muslims, the Islampur movement included. As of 2014, Garrison reported seventy movements to Christ in twenty-nine countries. He defined a movement as "100 new churches or 1000 baptisms that emerge/happen within a two-decade period." All of these seventy movements that he cited had begun in the last twenty years.[42] Anecdotally, these movements fall across the spectrum in terms of identity and association. This increase in movements represents a tremendous opportunity to evaluate and learn from God's work among Muslims, particularly in light of the questions this chapter has raised.[43]

As a field worker, I seek to learn from the ongoing research and insights. Yet I also have to sort out how I, as a foreign missionary, can faithfully announce Jesus' good news and relate to fellowships formed around that message. In my efforts to envision the goals for my own ministry of evangelism and discipleship and the prescriptive takeaways from the C Spectrum debate, I have come to resonate with the heart of Parshall's concern. In particular, both the C Spectrum and Parshall's writings pose the question: *How can believers be culturally and socially connected with their existing communities even as they embrace biblical norms that differ from that community?*

---

42 Garrison, *A Wind in the House of Islam: How God Is Drawing Muslims Around the World to Faith in Jesus Christ*, Location 135.

43 A short listing of some of the volumes to emerge recently shows the salient insights. Prenger has supplied insights into the thinking and practice of C5 leaders—thinking and practice which reflects great diversity on some of the key issues like the role of the mosque and the Quran. Prenger, *Muslim Insider Christ Followers: Their Theological and Missiological Frames*. Naja provides a detailed study of two movements in East Africa ("Sixteen Features"). Kraft studies Arab Muslim converts who self-describe as "Christians." See Kraft, *Searching for Heaven in the Real World: A Sociological Discussion of Conversion in the Arab World*. Multiple other volumes have emerged exploring the factors involved in Muslims coming to faith and the qualities of different movements to Christ, both in popular and academic forms. See David Greenlee, ed. *From the Straight Path to the Narrow Way: Journeys of Faith*; David Greenlee, ed. *Longing for Community*; David Watson and Paul Watson, *Contagious Disciple Making: Leading Others on a Journey of Discovery*; Nik Ripken and Gregg Lewis, *The Insanity of God: A True Story of Faith Resurrected*; Jerry Trousdale, *Miraculous Movements: How Hundreds of Thousands of Muslims Are Falling in Love with Jesus*. Talman and Travis, eds. *Understanding Insider Movements: Disciples of Jesus Within Diverse Religious Communities*; Gene Daniels and Warrick Farah, eds. *Margins of Islam: Ministry of Diverse Muslim Contexts*.

This is a fundamental missiological question, raised in multiple books and articles over centuries.[44]

I have tended, then, to see two primary "ditches" that believers and cross-cultural missionaries are trying to avoid. The first is the ditch of isolation. Too great a distance culturally from a community labels the gospel as colonial or foreign or outsider. We believe, however, that God has come near to every human community in the gospel. As Andrew Walls puts it, "God accepts us as we are," including who we are in our group relations.[45] On the other hand, we seek to avoid the ditch of ungodly compromise—a condition in which the distinctives of Jesus' lordship and exclusive saving work are minimized or lost. In pursuit of effective discipleship and biblically grounded churches, I propose that we all aim for a target space between these two ditches.

At the end of the day, there is a distinction between the ways a group of believers see their associations and disassociations: Do they align primarily with foreigners or an existing historic church? Do they still see themselves as Muslims, or something in between as Kim discussed in chapter 4.[46] But though these are important questions, they are ultimately symptomatic of the core issues of engagement, cultural isolation, and syncretistic accommodation, which are our primary concerns. Moreover, these two ditches can be manifested at any point on the C Spectrum. Those inclined to foreign culture also run the danger of subsuming Jesus' lordship under other authorities (including foreign culture itself). Those inclined toward local cultural norms can isolate themselves and become insular or ethnocentric, failing to obey Jesus' command to make disciples of all nations. One can envision a prescriptive scale that exposes the ditches of isolation and compromise on each side, but two-dimensional models like the C1-6 scale have their limitations. They further a binary perspective that has so frequently plagued these discussions. No particular pattern of discipleship or evangelism protects us from the dangers of syncretism, accommodation, or isolation.

Acknowledging these ditches helps us process the debate surrounding the C Spectrum. We recognize that there can be compromised groups which have not given full allegiance to Jesus' lordship. We also recognize the danger of a colonial or ethnocentric paradigm which co-opts local groups into foreign or majority languages and cultures. Therefore Parshall's advocacy for C4 communities seems to be an appropriate ideal of "church" in a Muslim community: Believers distinguish themselves for their faith commitments but aim to remain part of their community in some meaningful way. However, as I

---

44 See especially Walls, "The Gospel as Prisoner and Liberator of Culture."
45 Ibid., 7.
46 See my clarifications concerning the term and category "Muslim" earlier in the chapter. With ongoing caveats about "religious terms" still in place, I use the word here to reflect sociological, cultural, and ethnic categories of self-identification.

discussed above, we come to acknowledge that this ideal may be pursued at any position on Travis's C Spectrum, even as the dangerous ditches threaten each group on the spectrum. This allows us to retain the C Spectrum as a descriptive tool while still encouraging reflective inquiry into what marks "Christ-centered communities" and how missionaries contribute to their development.

This still leaves us with the hard work of ministry in context under Jesus' lordship. I live in a pioneer setting with few believers and no historic church. In this context, my role is to observe what God is doing across the Muslim world in the various expressions of faith emerging over the past twenty years, to discern my own context by listening respectfully and well to my community, and then to proclaim Jesus' love and authority in that context. For believers and seekers inclined toward foreign identification and foreign paradigms, we exalt Jesus as Lord of every community and Savior of all who believe, no matter what community they were born into. For those inclined to uncritical adaptation of birth culture to their new faith, we exalt Jesus' authority over all authorities, including the traditions they have received from the past. We evangelize and disciple based on context and the needs and tendencies of the seekers and believers we meet.

Based on conscience and calling, missionaries are drawn to different approaches regarding continuity of identity, culture, and language. This diversity is appropriate and necessary. It is part of the distinctive gifts that the Spirit has given Christ's body, including those involved in the missionary task. Though we study the Scriptures intently, live according to our consciences, and argue for our paradigms, the Holy Spirit leads in surprising ways. We are ultimately servants of the Lord—not of our paradigms and models. I have repeatedly met missionaries who aimed for a C3, C4, or C5 church, only to see a different kind of church emerge through the Spirit's leading within the contextual demands. God calls each community and each believer within his or her own context; and we need to respect that calling and the beautiful power of the Spirit to fulfill God's purposes for each community and the individuals within them. We must also be wary of hindering the gospel from reaching into new, unengaged communities because of biases developed outside (or inside) of the community context.

Cautions and Conclusion

In my current host country in Central Asia, I have observed an intense conflict between a modernist agenda and traditional values. Modernists are drawn to the West, including its impulses to secularism. Traditionalists seek to uphold traditional culture, often using Islamic terminology to do so, but not necessarily based on so-called Islamic orthodoxy. In many ways, this competition between modern and traditional runs through the very heart of families. City-dwelling families often lean one way, even as they have relatives in distant villages committed to another way. How do we speak the truth of the good news of Jesus' death and resurrection and glorious salvation for all (traditionalists and modernists included) who put their faith in him? Is Jesus only for traditionalists? Is Jesus only for modernists? Of course not. He is for all of the people of all nations and all peoples in all contexts (Rom 3:29–30). Our contextualization of that foundational message must not yoke the gospel message to one particular side in the ongoing conflict.

The huge temptation in each context is to universalize the experience of an individual believer or group of believers to all Muslims in that context or to all Muslim contexts. The reality is that even within the same country or people group, those who find Jesus come from a variety of perspectives. Some are traditionalists; some are inclined toward foreignness; and some lie somewhere in between. In my ministry, I engage some who have been drawn into the gospel message *because* of the positive words about Jesus in the Qur'an and the Hadiths. And I engage with others who are drawn to the gospel message because they were repulsed by the violence they saw as inherent to Islam. To universalize either of these experiences is to predecide where all Muslims will fall on the C Spectrum. I believe this is a mistake that has dominated the C Spectrum debate. Advocates of each point on the scale can point to some believer somewhere who shows the dangers of other points. As those engaging cross-culturally with the gospel, we must be careful lest we unintentionally hinder the Spirit's work in different contexts from our own.

It is my hope that in the next two decades of discussion on the C Spectrum, other models of analysis will continue to emerge. But most of all, I pray that non-Muslim background contributors to the discussion will prove to be peacemakers (blessed are they) as they help Muslim background believers to rightly debate and process their diverse experiences under the lordship of Christ. If we sow division and exasperate the historic tensions between peoples, we will not be living in accord with the gospel that we preach (Gal 5:13–15).

Phil Parshall modelled this reflective engagement. He did so by calling for a greater move toward Muslim contexts in terms of cultural behavior and even spiritual language. He did so by his polite engagement with those with whom he disagreed. He did so, most strikingly, by his "removal of the Fatwa"[47] against any suspicion of motives or faith among fellow missiologists and practitioners. We do well to follow Parshall's lead on this as the gospel penetrates new people groups among Muslims in deeper and wider ways over the next decades.

---

47 Parshall, "Lifting the Fatwa."

References

Ayub, E. 2009. "Observations and Reactions to Christians Involved in a New Approach to Mission." *St. Francis Magazine* 5 (5): 21–40.

Barth, F. 1969. "Introduction." In *Ethnic Groups and Boundaries: The Social Organization of Culture Difference*, edited by Fredrik Barth, 9–38. Oslo, Norway: Universites for laget.

———. 1994. "Enduring and Emerging Issues in the Analysis of Ethnicity." In *The Anthropology of Ethnicity: Beyond 'Ethnic Groups and Boundaries*, edited by Hans Vermeulen and Cora Govers, 11–32. Amsterdam, NL: Het Spinhuis.

Burrows, W. 2018. "Theological Ideals, Cross-Cultural Realities: Syncretism and Hybridity in Christian Culture Crossings." In *Traditional Rituals as Christian Worship: Dangerous Syncretism or Necessary Hybridity?* edited by R. Daniel Shaw and William R. Burrow, 20–36. Maryknoll, NY: Orbis.

Canfield, R. L. 1973. *Faction and Conversion in a Plural Society: Religious Alignments in the Hindu Kush*. Ann Arbor, MI: University of Michigan.

Corwin, G. 2007. "A Humble Appeal to C5/Insider Movement Muslim Ministry Advocates to Consider Ten Questions." *International Journal of Frontier Missiology* 24 (1): 5–20.

Daniels, G. 2018. "Conclusion: Learning from the Margins," In *Margins of Islam: Ministry in Diverse Muslim Contexts*. Pasadena, CA: William Carey Library.

Daniels, Gene and Warrick Farah, eds. 2018. *Margins of Islam: Ministry of Diverse Muslim Contexts*. Pasadena, CA: William Carey Library.

Dixon, R. 2009. "Moving on From the C1-C6 Spectrum." *St. Francis Magazine* 5 (4): 3–19.

———. 2016. "When C4 Is Not Biblical in Many Respects." https://biblicalmissiology. org/2020/10/07/when-c4-is-not-biblical-in-many-respects/

Duerksen, Darren T., and William A. Dyrness. 2019. *Seeking Church*. Carol Stream, IL: InterVarsity.

Farah, W. 2018. "How Muslims Shape and Use Islam: Towards a Missiological Understanding." In *Margins of Islam: Ministry of Diverse Muslim Contexts*, edited by Gene Daniels and Warrick Farah. Pasadena, CA: William Carey Library.

Garrison, D. 2014. *A Wind in the House of Islam: How God Is Drawing Muslims Around the World to Faith in Jesus Christ*. Monument, CO: Wigtake Resources LLC.

Geertz, C. 1971. *Islam Observed: Religious Development in Morocco and Indonesia*. Chicago: University of Chicago Press.

Greenlee, D., ed. 2005. *From the Straight Path to the Narrow Way: Journeys of Faith*. Waynesboro, GA: Authentic.

———, ed. 2013. *Longing for Community*. Pasadena, CA: William Carey Library.

Hiebert, P. G. 1987. "Critical Contextualization." *International Bulletin of Missionary Research* 11 (3), 104–12.

Higgins, K. 2009. "Speaking the Truth About Insider Movements: Addressing the Criticisms of Bill Nikides and 'Phil' Relative to the Article 'Inside What?'" *St. Francis Magazine* 5 (6): 61–86.

Higgins, K., R. Jameson, and H. Talman, 2015. "Myths and Misunderstandings About Insider Movements." In *Understanding Insider Movements: Disciples of Jesus Within Diverse Religious Communities*, edited by Harley Talman and John Jay Travis. Pasadena, CA: William Carey Library.

Hill, H. 2007. "The Effects of Using Local and Non-Local Terms in Mother-Tongue Scripture." *Missiology: An International Review* 24: 383–96.

Imbach, S. R. 1984. "Syncretism." In *Evangelical Dictionary of Theology*, edited by Walter A. Elwell, 1062. Grand Rapids: Baker.

Jenkins, P. 2011. *The Next Christendom: The Coming of Global Christianity*. New York: Oxford University Press.

Kraft, K. A. 2012. *Searching for Heaven in the Real World: A Sociological Discussion of Conversion in the Arab World*. Oxford: Regnum Books International.

Lingel, M., J. Morton, and B. Nikkedes, eds. 2012. *Chrislam: How Missionaries Are Promoting an Islamized Gospel*. i2 ministries.

Marranci, G. 2008. *The Anthropology of Islam* [Kindle Edition]. New York: Berg Publishers.

Moreau, A. S. 2000. "Syncretism." In *Evangelical Dictionary of World Missions*, edited by A. Scott Moreau, 924. Grand Rapids: Baker.

Morse, G. 2017. "Why Are So Many So Silent? The Insider Movement in America." https://www.desiringgod.org/articles/why-are-so-many-so-silent.

Morton, J. 2011. "Insider Movements and the Historical Approach." *Journal of Biblical Missiology*, February 8, 2011. http://biblicalmissiology.org/2011/02/08/insider-movements-and-the-historical-approach.

Naja, B. 2013. "A Jesus Movement Among Muslims: Research from Eastern Africa." *International Journal of Frontier Missiology* 30 (1): 27–29.

———. 2013. "Sixteen Features of Belief and Practice in Two Movements Among Muslims in Eastern Africa: What Does the Data Say?" *International Journal of Frontier Missiology* 30 (4): 155–60.

Nikides, B. 2009. "A Response to Kevin Higgins' 'Inside What? Church, Religion and Insider Movements in Biblical Perspective." *St. Francis Magazine* 5 (4): 92–113.

Nongbri, B. 2013. *Before Religion*. New Haven, CT: Yale University Press.

Parshall, P. 1980. *New Paths in Muslim Evangelism: Evangelical Approaches to Contextualization*. Grand Rapids: Baker.

———. 1998. "Danger! New Directions in Contextualization." *Evangelical Missions Quarterly* 34 (4): 404–6, 409–10.

———. 2004. "Lifting the Fatwa." *Evangelical Missions Quarterly* 40 (3): 288–93.

———. 2007. *Muslim Evangelism: Contemporary Approaches to Contextualization*. Colorado Springs, CO: Biblica.

Prenger, H. 2017. *Muslim Insider Christ Followers: Their Theological and Missiological Frames*. Pasadena, CA: William Carey Library.

Richard, H. L. 2014. "Religious Syncretism as a Syncretistic Concept: The Inadequacy of the 'World Religions' Paradigm in Cross-Cultural Encounter." *International Journal of Frontier Missiology* 31 (4): 209–14.

Ripken, N., and G. Lewis. 2013. *The Insanity of God: A True Story of Faith Resurrected.* Nashville: B&H Publishing.

Sanneh, L. 1996. *Translating the Message: The Missionary Impact on Culture.* Mary Knoll, NY: Orbis.

Sciortino, G. "Ethnicity, Race, Nationhood, Foreignness, and Many Other Things: Prolegomena to a Cultural Sociology of Difference-Based Interactions," In *The Oxford Handbook of Cultural Sociology,* edited by Ronald N. Jacobs, Jeffrey C. Alexander, and Philip Smith, 365–89. Oxford: Oxford University Press.

Shaw, R. D. 2010. "Beyond Contextualization: Toward a Twenty-First-Century Model for Enabling Mission." *International Bulletin of Missionary Research* 34 (4): 208–15.

———. 2018. "The Dynamics of Ritual and Ceremony: Transforming Traditional Rites to Their Intended Purpose." In *Traditional Rituals as Christian Worship: Dangerous Syncretism or Necessary Hybridity?* edited by R. D. Shaw and William R. Burrow, 1–19. Maryknoll, NY: Orbis.

Smith, J. 2009. "An Assessment of the Insider's Principle Paradigms." *St. Francis Magazine* 5 (4): 20–51.

Talman, H., and J. Travis, eds. 2015. *Understanding Insider Movements: Disciples of Jesus Within Diverse Religious Communities.* Pasadena, CA: William Carey Library.

Tennent, T. C. 2006. "Followers of Jesus (Isa) in Islamic Mosques: A Closer Examination of C-5 'High Spectrum' Contextualization." *International Journal of Frontier Missions* 23 (3): 101–15.

Travis, J. 1998. "The C1 to C6 Spectrum: A Practical Tool for Defining Six Types of 'Christ-centered Communities' ('C') Found in the Muslim Context." *Evangelical Missions Quarterly* 34 (4): 411–15.

———. 2015. "The C1-C6 Spectrum After Fifteen Years: Misunderstandings, Limitations, and Recommendations." In *Understanding Insider Movements: Disciples of Jesus Within Diverse Religious Communities,* edited by Harley Talman and John Jay Travis, 489–96. Pasadena, CA: William Carey Library.

Travis, J., and A. Travis. 2013. "Roles of 'Alongsiders' in Insider Movements." *International Journal of Frontier Missiology* 30 (4): 161–69.

Trousdale, J. 2012. *Miraculous Movements: How Hundreds of Thousands of Muslims Are Falling in Love with Jesus.* Nashville: Thomas Nelson.

Walls, A. F. 1996. "The Gospel as Prisoner and Liberator of Culture." In *The Missionary Movement in Christian History: Studies in the Transmission of Faith.* Maryknoll, NY: Orbis.

Watson, D., and P. Watson. 2014. *Contagious Disciple Making: Leading Others on a Journey of Discovery.* Nashville: Thomas Nelson.

Werbner, P. 2010. "Religious Identity," In *The Sage Handbook of Identities,* edited by Margaret Wetherell and Chandra Talpade Mohanty. Thousand Oaks, CA: SAGE Publications.

Woodberry, J. D, ed. 2011. *From Seed to Fruit: Global Trends, Fruitful Practices, and Emerging Issues Among Muslims.* Pasadena, CA: William Carey Library.

Wright, N. T. 2013. *Paul and the Faithfulness of God.* Minneapolis: Fortress.

LIVING CROSS-CULTURALLY IN MUSLIM CONTEXTS

John Jay Travis

Reflections on Key Themes in the Writings and Ministry of Phil Parshall

Phil and Julie Parshall lived a total of thirty-nine years among Muslims in Asia. Together they exemplified how to live cross-culturally with understanding and empathy while trying to find relevant and meaningful ways to make Jesus known. What they modeled, and what Phil wrote about in his many books and articles, is helpful to anyone today wishing to work among Muslims while giving an answer "for the hope that is within you … with gentleness and respect" (1 Pet 3:15 ESV).

Introduction

My wife and I moved to a Muslim-majority part of Southeast Asia in 1986. When we first arrived in what would become our home for the next twenty-two years, there were very few people, foreign or national, dedicated to living as proximate witnesses[1] among Muslims. We arrived initially carrying only four books. One of them was Phil Parshall's challenging work, *New Paths in Muslim Evangelism*. This landmark book crystalized much of the thinking on contextualization and new ministry approaches that scholars and practitioners had discussed during the previous decade.[2]

We had first met Phil at our home church before moving overseas. His words captured our imagination. Because I had lived in a Muslim household

---

1 I use this term to refer to those who are proximate to (living near or with) Muslims, intentionally witnessing or sharing the good news of Jesus.
2 In the 1970s, Fuller Seminary, where Parshall studied, began its innovative Islamic Studies program under the leadership of Dudley Woodberry; during the landmark 1978 North American Conference on Muslim Evangelism, held in Colorado, Christian anthropologists and linguistics such as Paul Hiebert, Charles Kraft, Darrell Whiteman, Eugene Nida, and Charles Taber stressed the importance of engaging deeply with a people to understand their worldview and faith from an insider, or emic, point of view. All of this encouraged moves toward contextualized ministry in Muslim contexts.

in Southeast Asia during my university years, I was sure that the traditional ways of following Jesus that Western Christians talked about would not make a lot of sense to the Muslims I knew. Now here we were meeting a man who had already spent twenty years living among Muslims in Bangladesh and the Philippines, pioneering new ways of sharing about and following *Isa al-Masih* (Jesus the Messiah). As Phil shared that day at our church, my wife and I felt that we had met an older brother—a role model for us, who might have some of the answers we were looking for.

In the years following that first meeting, we eventually met Julie and had the privilege of getting to know both of the Parshalls better. Phil is a prolific writer, and we began studying his many books and articles.[3] In fact, just last month I finished reading Parshall's memoirs[4] and used another of his books[5] in a class I recently taught at Fuller Seminary.

The world, including the Muslim world, has changed significantly over the past forty years. When Phil wrote *New Paths in Muslim Evangelism* there were no cell phones or internet, personal computers were uncommon, relatively few cross-cultural workers were living among Muslims, and very few movements to Jesus were taking place. Yet, in spite of change, certain dynamics of cross-cultural living among Muslims have remained the same.

In 2007, Woodberry, Shubin, and Marks reported on survey research they had conducted with approximately 750 Muslims who had become followers of Jesus.[6] Their research indicated that the number-one factor that influenced these Muslims to follow Christ was the lifestyle of Jesus followers they had personally known.[7] Woodberry, Shubin, and Marks stated:

> A North African former Sufi mystic noted with approval that there was no gap between the moral profession and the practice of Christians he saw. An Egyptian contrasted the love of a Christian group at an American university with the unloving treatment of Muslim students and faculty he encountered at a university in Medina. An Omani woman explained that Christians treat women as equals. Others noted loving Christian marriages. Some poor people said the expatriate Christian workers they knew had adopted, contrary to their expectations, a simple lifestyle, wearing local clothes and observing local customs of not eating pork, drinking alcohol, or touching those of the opposite sex.[8]

---

3 See the appendix for a list of Phil Parshall's works.

4 *Divine Threads within a Human Tapestry*. This is a very moving and honest account of Phil and Julie's deep experiences with God and with Muslims while they were ministering in Asia. To this day we continue to be impacted by Phil's writings and reflections on how we as Jesus followers can and should live as witnesses among Muslims.

5 Parshall, *Bridges to Islam*.

6 Woodberry, Shubin, and Marks, "Why Muslims Follow Jesus."

7 The second factor was miraculous answers to prayer such as healing in the name of Jesus.

8 Woodberry, Shubin, and Marks, "Why Muslims Follow Jesus," 82.

Through his writings, Phil Parshall has much to say on this matter of the lifestyle of a follower of Jesus who lives among Muslims—culturally, materially, and spiritually.[9] Here I will highlight a number of the lifestyle dynamics and themes Parshall brings out, touching on subjects from language and culture to attitudes and spiritual life. I will add my own reflections and insights as well, which are based on years of personal experience living among Muslims.[10]

Friendship

The theme of friendship and the importance of relationship-building is found throughout Parshall's writings and is at the heart of any discussion on cross-cultural living. I have always appreciated stories Phil told of the close, life-long friendship he has had with Dr. Ali, a Bengali professor of Sufi studies.[11] This friendship continued years after the Parshalls left South Asia; and today Phil and Julie are still involved in the lives of Dr. Ali's children. Generally speaking, I have observed that those who have friends from the new culture (such as Phil's friendship with Dr. Ali) do well in cross-cultural living; conversely, those who do not make cross-cultural friends are likely to feel strange, awkward, or even hostile toward the new culture.

In her seminal work, *Joyful Witness in the Muslim World*, the late Dr. Evelyne Reisacher combines the biblical concept of joy with current research from neuroscience known as attachment theory.[12] Attachment theory begins by looking at how infants bond or attach to loving caregivers/parents in healthy ways, allowing the caregiver and infant together to experience a shared joy. In workshops on how to build friendships with Muslims, Reisacher emphasized the following:

> Given that joy is a primary attachment emotion, I recommend the obvious: first start to enjoy Muslims as human beings, to delight in them; this is how the bond will form, as it did when we first learn to attach to our caregivers as human beings. As joy is necessary in the formation of the bond in early childhood, so it continues to be important in the formation and growth of human bonds throughout life.[13]

Even though Reisacher very much longed for her Muslim friends to know Jesus, she railed against building friendships only for the purpose of talking about spiritual matters. Her entire book speaks of how, in many spheres of life

---

9   See, in particular, *New Paths in Muslim Evangelism*, 97–125; *Bridges to Islam*, 113–43; and "Lessons Learned in Contextualization," 251–65.
10 We lived twenty-two years in Southeast Asia, two years in South Asia, and have traveled extensively in other Muslim-majority parts of Asia, the Middle East, and Africa.
11 See *Divine Threads within a Human Tapestry*, 59, 133–35.
12 Reisacher, *Joyful Witness in the Muslim World*.
13 Ibid., 29.

(e.g., the arts, in nature, helping the poor), Muslims and Christians can and should build meaningful relationships.

Unfortunately, in building cross-cultural relationships, we seldom begin with a clean slate. The past impacts the present for good or for bad. Parshall's writings, therefore, stress the need not only to understand differing cultural and religious cross-cultural factors, but also the historical, political, and socioeconomic realities that have shaped a people's present-day identity.

Parshall reminds Westerners living cross-culturally among Muslims how the imperialism, colonialism, and racism of the recent past has set Muslims on edge against the "Christian" West; indeed, at the onset of World War II almost all traditional Muslim homelands were in some way under European ("Christian") domination.[14] This legacy of imperialism, economic exploitation, and racism is, to this day, part of the collective memory of many Muslims. In addition, Westerners living among Muslims need to distance themselves from the assumed immoral lifestyle of the "Christian West," a perception in part created by and also reinforced by Hollywood.

Cultural Bonding

Building a true cross-cultural friendship is seldom quick or simple. It takes time, humility, and a continual learning posture. One way this can happen is to follow the teaching of Tom and Betty Sue Brewster in what they call "bonding"—a way to acquire cultural savvy and language skills, as well as new cross-cultural relationships.[15]

Bonding is what many today might call an extended "homestay," where one lives a month or longer with a family in a cross-cultural situation. By living with a family and allowing the natural closeness that living under one roof tends to create, one "bonds," or forms close connections, with not only one family, but by extension, often with the surrounding community as well.

I have lived with families cross-culturally on four occasions. Sharing meals—relaxing together and identifying with each other's daily routines—does a lot to break down walls and help us see religious others as friends. Talking by candlelight when the electricity goes out, running to the hospital to visit a sick family member, affectionately being given a fitting local name—these types of things can happen in a bonding situation.

---

14 At the onset of World War II, most of today's independent Muslim-majority countries were in some way under the colonial or administrative rule of England, France, Holland, or Russia—all countries seen as "Christian" in the eyes of the colonized. Also see Parshall, *The Last Great Frontier*, 449.

15 See Brewster and Brewster, *Bonding and the Missionary Task*.

During the time we lived in Southeast Asia, over thirty cross-cultural workers from six different countries worked on teams with us. Some came from neighboring Asian countries and others from Western contexts. In all cases, each of our teammates, whether single or a family, spent at least the first month in the country bonding with a Muslim family.[16] The results were extraordinary: People would often come out of their bonding experience feeling like they not only knew one family well but had become acquainted with many others in the extended family and community as well.[17] Some lifelong cross-cultural friendships, similar to that of Phil Parshall and Dr. Ali, were formed. And the blessing generally went both ways—Muslim families appreciated having cross-cultural Christian friends as well.

Bonding didn't take place just with foreign workers. In time, a number of national Christians had learned of the non-governmental organization (NGO) work we were doing in Muslim communities in Southeast Asia and wanted to join us. Some of them came from Bible schools to do internships with our NGO. We told them that if they wanted to work with us there were certain lifestyle adjustments they would need to make in dress, diet, religious terminology, and related matters. We also required them to live with a Muslim family for one month, just as the foreign cross-cultural workers had done.

One of the first of these national Christians who wanted join our NGO was absolutely flabbergasted at our request that he go live temporarily with a Muslim family. He said to us, "You guys can't be serious! I was born here—this is my language! If you foreigners do this, well, it makes sense; you need to learn the language and culture. But what sense does this make for me?"

I politely tried to explain our experience and point out some of what he might learn as a Christian, even having been born in the same country, during the time he would live with a Muslim family. Eventually he agreed to give it a try. He soon found a lovely older Muslim couple whose children had already grown up and left the home, and he rented a room from them. He loved them and they loved him. After one month he asked the NGO leadership if he could spend the entire six months of the internship living with this Muslim family!

The Parshalls didn't live with a family when they first arrived in Bangladesh in 1962. (They preceded the Brewsters' bonding article by thirty years!)

---

16 Depending on the circumstances, I would sometimes arrange a family ahead of time for our teammates. For single women on our team, we took great care to make sure the bonding family would offer good support and social protection.

17 In *Bonding and the Missionary Task*, the Brewsters recommend living with a local family from the religious and cultural group one is trying to bond with from one's first few days in country. Others have recommended this type of bonding after an initial six months of language learning (unless one already speaks the language). Both approaches have their strengths and weaknesses.

However, they did have a living situation where they bonded with people in a rural area of Bangladesh. They lived their first five years in a small, simple village home with no electricity or running water. Just living in such a community gave them tremendous opportunities to become acquainted with many families.

This raises an important point about bonding. If, for whatever reason, one cannot find a bonding situation, other approaches may need to be tried in order to have meaningful community interaction and immersion. The point is this: Life happens in and around homes and families. To build friendships and understand another culture, the closer we are to households, the more we will understand and feel part of the community.

Home and Hospitality

Since so much happens in and around the home, Parshall had much to say about one's choice of residence, including its size and location and the lifestyle taking place within it—for example, dress, diet, house pets, and how guests are received. All of this matters in living cross-culturally long-term.[18]

Muslims are renowned for their hospitality. No matter their economic status, whatever Muslim families own in terms of furniture and artwork, the best they have will be placed in the front room where guests are received. Upon entering a home, visitors are made to feel like guests of honor, with drinks immediately served and snacks coming shortly thereafter. Does one's home feel welcoming to guests? Do neighbors feel free to drop by to chat or borrow some sugar? Something even as simple as a choice of pet can be either welcoming or off-putting. Although it varies somewhat from country to country, in general Muslims view dogs as unclean and defiling. Cats, on the other hand, are acceptable.

Diet

Diet also matters. Muslims have very strict rules regarding halal food. In the first week in our home (where we ended up living for eighteen years), our house helper[19] was discretely approached by the neighbors as she took out the trash. We lived on a narrow street, just wide enough for one car to pass, and we shared common walls with our neighbors. The neighbors asked our helper, "Hey, do they have alcohol in the house? Are they eating pork? Is their food halal?" There were no secrets on that street!

---

18 See Parshall, *New Paths in Muslim Evangelism*, 110–17; and Parshall, *The Last Great Frontier*, 315–20.

19 We lived in a lower- to middle-class urban neighborhood. All of our neighbors had house help or at least younger or poorer family members from the village whom they employed to work for them. If we did not have house help, we would have been viewed as stingy, as we would have been depriving someone of a good job.

Fortunately, our house helper was able to say, "No alcohol and no pork."[20] Our neighbors were not simply curious; there was actually a larger and more practical matter in their minds: If we invited them over to our home to eat, would they be defiled by our food? Or even if the food in front of them was halal, were our plates and glasses "unclean" (i.e., had they ever been used to serve alcohol, pork, or other non-halal foods)? In other words, even though we were not Muslims, were we at least "safe" to visit?

Dress

Like food, dress is also crucial.[21] Unfortunately, many assumptions and judgments are quickly made based on appearance. The question often arises regarding whether or not cross-cultural workers should wear Muslim dress. The issue is more immediately relevant for women, due to the common practices of covering the head, maintaining certain standards of modesty such as wearing long sleeves, or covering the face when outside the home.

Like so many aspects of lifestyle, what is right depends on context. When my wife and I were staying in a rural part of Afghanistan, she wore the blue burka from head to toe outside the home. To do otherwise would be insulting and improper, if not dangerous. In the capital city of Kabul, however, she simply wore a long tunic, long pants, and a light head scarf similar to what many urban Afghan women wore.

When we lived in Southeast Asia, my wife wore colorful Muslim-style tunics and long pants. Westerners typically wore clothing that they considered to be modest, but their clothing was often deemed inappropriate by local Muslims. Indeed, the media provides ample exposure for various styles of dress. Yet, at the same time many Muslims would assume that the person so dressed could not be very serious about God. A neighbor of ours advised my wife to continue to dress as she did (different than the typical foreign mode of dress). She said the women in the community felt safe around her, since the way she dressed did not make them feel awkward when their husbands saw her.

In some Muslim contexts, if a man can grow a beard it is important for him to do so. But what style of beard should he grow? What kind of jewelry would a respectable person wear? Does makeup communicate a message? In some places, footwear is a crucial factor. In what social context is it appropriate for a host or guest to be dressed casually? When might casual dress be insulting? What defines casual dress versus formal dress? These social mores can vary so much from place to place that the cross-cultural worker needs to learn not only by observing but by interacting with local Muslims about their views of dress.

---

20 The Parshalls were profoundly aware of the importance of keeping a halal diet when living in Muslim contexts. (See chapter 1 and the table in this chapter.)
21 See Parshall, *New Paths in Muslim Evangelism*, 114–16.

Language and Religious Vocabulary

Due to the effects of globalization, the internet, and a nearly universal desire to be proficient in English, some cross-cultural workers have assumed it is preferable to minister in English. I imagine that in some contexts this may be true. But something very profound happens when we learn the language of the other and learn it well. In his memoirs, Phil speaks of doing language studies in Bangladesh for nine hours a day!

For many people, one of the most precious aspects of their heritage is their language. Bridges are built when we can communicate with people in their heart language. And more bridges can be built when we know their religious and spiritual vocabulary as well. Where we lived in Southeast Asia, Muslims called Jesus *Isa* and Christians called him *Yesus*. When we used the name *Yesus*, conversations tended to be short; we could talk for hours with neighbors and friends, however, about *Isa al-Masih* (Jesus the Messiah). Parshall stresses the need to communicate with Muslims using the religious vocabulary with which they are familiar and comfortable.[22]

Bringing together a number of dynamics we have discussed this far, including language, a good friend of mine who works in a rural setting in Asia shared a fascinating insight. The town where he works is entirely Muslim, and he mastered both the local language and one of the broadly spoken regional languages. The name given to him by his neighbors is their form of his English name (a name found in both the Bible and the Quran). He always makes it clear that he is a follower of Jesus, and shares openly about his spiritual life. Yet when the locals talk about my friend, they describe him as a good Muslim!

The first time he heard this, he was surprised. He said, "Guys, you don't see me in the mosque, and I've never said that I'm a Muslim. In fact, I have always made it clear that I follow Isa." They answered, "We know all that. But with your name, where you live, how you dress, and *especially the fact that you speak the language of our hearts*—well, the only term we have for a person like you—is Muslim."

Meaningful Bible Translations

Related to language and religious vocabulary is also the choice of a Bible translation by those who give witness to Jesus. There are multiple translations of the Bible in many of the major Muslim languages of the world today. Some use religious vocabulary much more in keeping with the common language of the Muslim population. The names of prophets, divine names, and terms

---

22 See Parshall, "Lessons Learned in Contextualization," 254–55, 264, where he discusses the use of Isa and Allah in witness among Muslims and in Bible translations.

used to identify holy books can either help draw Muslim readers into Scripture or be off-putting. In Bangladesh Parshall saw the tremendous impact a Bible translation had when it used Isa al-Masih for Jesus and other such words with which Muslims feel comfortable.[23] Cross-cultural witnesses should become familiar with Scripture verses and stories using translations that affectively and cognitively speak reality to native Muslim speakers of that language.[24]

Values and "Goodness"

Most assume that what makes someone "good" should be obvious. Any monocultural group can fairly quickly come up with a list of the top three or four traits that describe goodness. What happens, though, when another cultural group comes up with a different list? It quickly becomes clear that values—those traits deemed as most important—are often culturally specific.[25]

When I lived in Southeast Asia, I would often ask Muslim friends to describe for me a good person. I consistently heard essentially the same answer, which went something like this: "A good person is patient, never gets angry, and generous with money and time." When I asked my American Christian friends this question, they would tend to say something like this: "A good person is honest, hard-working, and morally pure." Although Muslims in Southeast Asia also appreciate honesty, hard work, and moral purity, these are not the first attributes that come to mind.

Which list, from a biblical perspective, is correct? The Bible actually encourages both. Therefore we need—for the sake of our witness and cross-cultural relationships—to "contextualize" goodness. If we fail to do this (which I have been guilty of plenty of times!), we can be seen as clueless and childish at best, and rude and uncaring at worst.

There is no monolithic Islamic culture, yet in Muslim-majority areas where I have spent time, hospitality and generosity seem to be two widely embraced values. Westerners, unfortunately, can often seem stingy to Muslims. Most Christian cross-cultural workers wouldn't want to appear extravagant or flippant with money, and some are afraid of being taken advantage of. Yet knowing the inherent risks of being misunderstood or coming across

---

23 Parshall, "Lessons Learned in Contextualization," 264.

24 Besides *Isa al-Masih*, these translations would likely use *Yahya* for John the Baptist and *Maryam* (rather than a form of "Maria") for Mary the mother of Jesus. For over twenty years, I have collected Bibles from around the world that use *Isa*. Some examples of significant languages spoken by Muslims today that have at least one translation using *Isa* includes Arabic, Turkish, Indonesian, Somali, Persian (Farsi), Madurese, Pattani Malay, Pashto, Uzbek, Tajik, Urdu, Kazakh, and Balochi. Many of these translations also use *Allah* or other terms for God that are commonly used by Muslims of that language group.

25 See Elmer, *Cross-Cultural Conflict*, for excellent insights on how various behaviors and traits are viewed as less or more important, depending on the culture.

as stingy rather than generous, a friend of mine who worked in a very poor Muslim community in West Africa has been known to say, "I'd rather be had than be hard."

I had an experience that illustrated this reality for me. There were about forty homes in the neighborhood where we lived. One day a small delegation visited my house to collect money for repaving the street. I invited the group in, had tea served, and we chatted informally. When I saw the official folder in their hands, I realized that this small delegation, consisting of my friends and neighbors, was going from house to house collecting funds. As they described the merits of the project, I was trying to gauge what an appropriately generous amount to give would be. So I asked in roundabout ways what the rest of the neighbors were giving. They gave me a range of amounts, concluding with "except for our five community bosses."

I could tell from the way they used the word *boss* that they meant someone they viewed as able to give more than most and who had a sincere interest in the welfare of the community. So I discreetly asked how much the bosses were giving, assuming I should give something between what most neighbors were giving and the expected "boss" contribution. They told me how much four of the five bosses were giving. When I asked who the fifth boss was, they acted a bit surprised, yet smiling broadly they said, "Well, brother John, you are our fifth boss!"

It was a humorous moment. I was not being taken advantage of; I was honored to be viewed as an integral part of the community. Gladly I gave an amount commensurate with being a boss!

Parshall recounts a very touching story involving the generosity of both money and time, mixed with heartfelt compassion. He was racing home with his car full of food for an important meal that evening at his house for fellow Christian workers. He recalls the drive home:

> In a fleeting moment, I saw a form with crumpled clothes in a fetal position lying by the side of the road. Bangladesh was, at that time, in the grip of a Book of Lamentations–type famine. Villagers had come by the tens of thousands to Dhaka to either find employment or beg. Literally scores swooned in the streets from malnutrition.
>
> In the next few seconds as I sped by, many contradictory thoughts bombarded my mind. "Yes, I am in a hurry; no, not in that big of a hurry. He is one of hundreds; he is important to God. I am a 'priest'; I am about to pass by on the other side [of the street]. My wife is going to make the feast tonight; this guy is starving. I have nice clothes; he has rags. I am warm and dry; he is soaked to the skin and cold. I have hope; he has no hope."

Brakes applied. Sliding to a stop, I reversed, got out in the rain and helped an amazed creation of God get into the car. At our home he was fed, clothed, and put to bed. Next morning, we gave him money and urged him to return to his loved ones in the village.[26]

Spiritual Life

In multiple articles, Parshall addresses the spiritual life of cross-cultural witnesses working among Muslims. In addition to addressing how we, as followers of Jesus, are to love God wholeheartedly and others as we love ourselves, he also asks how our Muslim friends and associates might perceive our spiritual life.

Based on a survey Parshall administered in the 1980s to roughly four hundred cross-cultural workers in regard to their spiritual lives, he concluded we always need to be upgrading in the areas of regularly encountering God through prayer and Bible study. Parshall mentioned famous missionaries of the past such as Hudson Taylor and Adoniram Judson who were "permeated by spiritual priorities" and whose "lives were a penetrating reflection of their relationship with Christ."[27]

Parshall, an advocate and pioneer in the area of contextualization, then went on to say, "Perhaps our technological age has seduced us into thinking that contextualized methodology is a more pressing area of emphasis than is our spiritual encounter with our Lord."[28] If this was true in the 1980s when technology was less advanced and contextual methodologies were only beginning to be tried, I would have to believe Parshall's words speak to us even more today.

Some of Parshall's strongest admonitions regarding spiritual life, however, are his comments on marriage and moral purity. In "The Tiger of Lust,"[29] Parshall pleads with fellow workers to be radical in turning away from lust, pornography, and any hint of improper relationships outside of marriage. With the pervasiveness of the internet and readily available pornography, I believe Parshall's words ring home today all the more.

Parshall also refers to "incarnated spirituality." By this he means prayer and the living out of spirituality in such a way that Muslims could appreciate and begin to engage in meaningful spiritual interactions with a follower of Jesus.

One of Parshall's most well-known stories regarding incarnated spirituality (or the lack thereof) occurred in an encounter he had with the President of Bangladesh. The President was well-acquainted with a Pentecostal missionary named Cal Olson.

26 *Divine Threads within a Human Tapestry*, 78.
27 "Lessons Learned in Contextualization," 263.
28 Ibid.
29 *The Last Great Frontier*, 291–94.

Phil referred to this missionary as "Saint Cal" due to his extended times of prayer, intense times of fasting, and continual talk about God and spiritual matters. The President, a Muslim, had previously rented a house he owned to Cal. Observing Cal's life, the President was very impressed with Cal's "mystical Christianity."[30]

The President traveled a lot and wanted to rent out the bottom floor of his home to someone he could trust. He contacted Cal. Cal declined, but introduced Phil to the President, knowing Phil was in need of office space. After sharing sweets and tea at the President's home, a lease was agreed upon between Phil and the President. In fact, the President even allowed a Bible Correspondence School to be located on the first floor!

On one occasion when the former president was back from his travels, he stopped by the house to see Phil. Sitting together, the president turned to Phil and with penetrating eyes asked him, "Mr. Parshall, are you a man of God like my good friend, Mr. Olson?"

Parshall says he just stared back, thinking to himself, "How do I even begin to respond?" Before giving much of a response, the former president followed up his first question with the following words: "Actually, Mr. Parshall, you remind me more of an American diplomat than you do a man of God like Mr. Olson."

Parshall quickly excused himself from the painful situation. He reflected on this interaction and went on to write: "My desire [is to] so live out my faith that Muslims would recognize me as having a spiritual dynamic that would draw them to the savior. The reality, at least to the president [was that] I was articulate, informed, and very American."[31]

This experience caused Parshall to try to look at spirituality in terms of lifestyle and forms. Some of his observations are found in the following table.[32]

Local Muslim Leader	Cross-Cultural Western Worker
Passive disposition	A driver, a doer
Subjective in outlook	Objective in orientation to life
People-oriented	Task-oriented
Financially poor (with the exception of certain *pirs*)	Possessor of a car, camera, computer, tape recorder, etc.; regarded as extremely rich
Would not attend drama, watch TV, or go to movies	Would do all of these

30 Ibid., 113.
31 *Divine Threads within a Human Tapestry*, 113–14.
32 From Parshall, *The Last Great Frontier*, 457

Would not eat in expensive restaurants	Would eat in expensive restaurants
Would not eat pork	Would eat pork
Man's clothes identify him as a religious person	Clothes identify him as a secular person
Wears a beard	Infrequently has a beard
Wife would either wear a veil or culturally approved clothes	Female workers have not always dressed in clothes which would be regarded by Muslims as modest; thus they are identified with the "sinful" characters seen on Western movie and TV import.

In the neighborhood where we lived for so many years, we searched for ways to share our spiritual life with those around us. The first was through praying with Muslims for healing. We have prayed with many Muslims, both for physical healing and inner healing.[33] Only once has a Muslim ever declined our offer to pray.

Second, when we prayed with Muslims, we would make it clear that healing is not accomplished by us but by God. In fact, our example in prayer for healing is Jesus. Therefore, using a Bible translation that incorporates the spiritual language Muslims are familiar with, we would often read an example of Jesus' healing, such as Peter's mother-in-law who suffered from a fever (Matt 8:14–15; Mark 1:29–31; Luke 4:38–39), or the bleeding woman (Matt 9:20–22; Mark 5:25–34; Luke 8:43–48). As Woodberry, Shubin, and Mark's research that I referred to earlier indicates the second-most common reason why Muslims turn to Jesus is because of a miraculous, Jesus-centered encounter with God.[34]

Third, we freely talked about spiritual experiences we were having with God or about miraculous answers to prayer. When the moment was right, we would speak about seeing people set free from *jinn*, or demons, in the name of Isa. We found that our Muslim friends didn't like talking about religion per se, but they loved talking about spirituality.

Finally, as we prayed with Muslims, since we believe there is not a single correct or "biblical" prayer posture, we would pray in whatever form made Muslims feel comfortable in an attempt to follow Parshall's advice to "incarnate" spirituality. If our friends wanted to kneel on their living room

---

33 See Travis and Travis, "Deep Level Healing Prayer in Cross-Cultural Ministry" for a discussion of the theory and practice of inner healing prayer in cross-cultural contexts. My wife and I have had the opportunity to engage in inner healing prayer with Muslims and Muslim-background followers of Jesus in numerous Asian, Middle Eastern, and North African countries.
34 Woodberry, Shubin, and Marks, "Why Muslims Follow Jesus."

rugs, we would kneel alongside them. If they wanted to pray with eyes open, that is what we did. If they wanted to pray in private, we looked for such a place. In short, we tried to bring the power of God into their lives in ways that they could embrace, with the hope that a time of prayer could open the way to further spiritual interactions.

Calling

Having a sense of being called by God for a specific task is a final theme that runs through several of Parshall's writings. He points out that by knowing God called him and Julie to live and minister cross-culturally among Muslims, it was easier to say yes or no to different invitations and job offers that came their way over the years. And there were quite a few such offers. Their sense of calling also gave them the perseverance they needed to hang on even in very difficult times.

Many struggle with the terms "calling" and "hearing from God," in large part because few of us have ever audibly heard the voice of God or an angel! Yet this very lack of being able to hear an audible voice is what causes us to seek God all the more in prayer and in Scripture and in trying to perceive that "still small voice" within (1 Kings 19:12 NKJV). Most of us sense God urging us toward something, and so we do it. We often check along the way, however, to make sure we are on the right track. God often makes his way clear to us for a period of time, even many decades, but at some point he may lead us in another direction.

The Lord led the Parshalls to live cross-culturally for nearly four decades. Phil closed his memoirs with the following:

> To the question, "Has it all been worthwhile?" comes a resounding positive response. I cannot imagine any other direction of life that could have possibly been as fulfilling, joyful or satisfying as that which I have chosen.
>
> And, so, the "final word" is simply an invitation to the reader to prayerfully consider a commitment to involvement in the Muslim World.
>
> "Oh, that the world of Islam may taste and see that the Lord is good."[35]

---

35 *Divine Threads within a Human Tapestry,* 209.

References

Brewster, T. and Brewster, E. 1982. *Bonding and the Missionary Task: Establishing a sense of belonging; Language learning is communication--is ministry!* Pasadena, CA: Lingua House.

Elmer, D. 1993. *Cross-Cultural Conflict: Building Relationships for Effective Ministry.* Downers Grove, IL: Intervarsity.

Parshall, P. 1980. *New Paths in Muslim Evangelism: Evangelical Approaches to Contextualization.* Grand Rapids: Baker.

———. 1983. *Bridges to Islam: A Christian Perspective on Folk Islam.* Grand Rapids: Baker.

———. 1989. "Lessons Learned in Contextualization." In *Muslims and Christians on the Emmaus Road,* edited by Dudley Woodberry, 251–65. Monrovia, CA: Missions Advanced Research.

———. 2000a. *The Last Great Frontier.* Quezon City, Philippines: Open Doors.

———. 2000b. *Divine Threads within a Human Tapestry: Memoirs of Phil Parshall.* Pasadena, CA: William Carey Library.

Reisacher, E. 2016. *Joyful Witness in the Muslim World: Sharing the Gospel in Everyday Encounters.* Grand Rapids: Baker Academic.

Travis, J. 2006. "Producing and Using Meaningful Translations of the *Taurat, Zabur* and *Injil.*" *International Journal of Frontier Missiology* 23 (2): 73-77.

Travis, J., and A. Travis. 2008. "Deep Level Healing Prayer in Cross-Cultural Ministry." In *Paradigm Shifts in Christian Witness: Insights from Anthropology, Communication and Spiritual Power,* edited by Charles Van Engen, et al., 106–15. Maryknoll, NY: Orbis.

Woodberry, D., R. Shubin, and G. Mark. 2007. "Why Muslims Follow Jesus." *Christianity Today,* October 24, 2007.

ABOUT THE
CONTRIBUTORS
AND EDITORS

MIRIAM ADENEY holds degrees from Wheaton College (BA), Syracuse University (MA), and Washington State University (PhD). She is an anthropologist and missiologist, a well-known writer, and has spoken on six continents. She is a past president of the American Society of Missiology, has been a plenary speaker at Missionexus and Evangelical Mission Society, and is a recipient of lifetime achievement awards from Media Associates International and Christians for Biblical Equality. Miriam is a professor at Seattle Pacific University. Among her books are *Daughters of Islam: Building Bridges with Muslim Women; Refugee Diaspora; Kingdom Without Borders: The Untold Story of Global Christianity;* and *God's Foreign Policy: Practical Ways to Help the World's Poor.*

GARY R. CORWIN received an MA from East Stroudsburg University (History), an MDiv from Trinity Evangelical Divinity School (Missions), and an MA from Northwestern University (African Studies). He is a missiologist, author, and editor, having served with SIM for thirty-eight years and as an editor and columnist for *EMQ* for twenty-three years. Gary is the author/editor of *By Prayer to the Nations: A Short History of SIM* (2018) and a coauthor of *Introducing World Missions: A Biblical, Historical, and Practical Survey* (2004, 2014).

KEVIN HIGGINS served with movements to Jesus in the Muslim world in two countries in South Asia. He received a PhD in 2013 from Fuller's School of Intercultural Studies in the area of translation. He currently serves as the General Director of Frontier Ventures.

ENOCH JINSIK KIM earned a PhD at Fuller Theological Seminary, where he is currently an associate professor in Communication and Mission Studies and the chairperson of the Korean Doctor of Missiology program. His publications include *Mission Strategy in the City* (Pickwick) and *Receptor-Oriented Communication for Hui Muslims in China* (ASM Monograph Series).

KENNETH NEHRBASS holds a PhD from Biola University and is an associate professor of intercultural studies at Biola University. He is also a translation and anthropology consultant with the Summer Institute of Linguistics (SIL) and The Seed Company. In addition to writing articles for *EMQ, Missiology, The Bible Translator, On Knowing Humanity, The Christian Education Journal, The Melanesian Journal of Theology*, and *The Great Commission Research Journal*, Kenneth is the author of several books, including *Advanced Missiology* (Cascade), *God's Image and Global Cultures* (Cascade) and *Christianity and Animism in Melanesia* (William Carey Library).

HARLEY TALMAN holds a PhD from Fuller School of Intercultural Studies and a ThM from Dallas Theological Seminary. He has served among Muslims for four decades in various capacities: church planting, theological education, field leadership, and humanitarian work. In addition to writing numerous articles, he teaches Islamic studies at a university in the US, as well as internationally.

JOHN JAY TRAVIS received a PhD from Fuller Theological Seminary, an MA in Intercultural Studies from Biola University, and an MA in TESOL from William Carey International University. He has spent more than twenty-five years working in Muslim-majority communities in South and Southeast Asia. John has published articles on a wide range of topics, including healing prayer, insider movements, contextualization, and Bible translation. Currently he teaches as affiliate faculty in the Fuller School of Intercultural Studies and is coeditor of the book *Understanding Insider Movements: Disciples of Jesus in Diverse Religious Communities* (William Carey Library, 2015).

JOSEPH S. WILLIAMS holds a DMiss from Biola University. For the past fifteen years he has ministered among Muslims in Central Asia. He has published articles in *St. Francis Magazine, Missiology*, and the *Great Commission Research Journal*.

MARK S. WILLIAMS earned a PhD in Development Studies at Ateneo de Davao University (Philippines) while serving in ministry to Muslims for twenty years (1990–2010) with SIM in the Philippines. He published articles in the *Journal of Asian Mission* and *Missiology*, and was a contributing author in *Missionary Methods: Research, Reflections, and Realities*, edited by C. Ott and J. D. Payne (William Carey Library, 2013).

# Appendix
Academic Works
by Phil Parshall

1975. *The Fortress and the Fire: Jesus Christ and the Challenge of Islam.* Bombay: Gospel Literature Service.

1977. "A Small Family Is a Happy Family." *Evangelical Missions Quarterly* 13 (4): 210.

1979. "Contextualized Baptism for Muslim Converts." *Missiology* 7 (4): 501–15.

1979. "Evangelizing Muslims: Are There Ways?" *Christianity Today* 23 (7): 28.

1980. *New Paths in Muslim Evangelism.* Grand Rapids: Baker.

1981. "An Empirical Appreciation of Muslim Community in Bangladesh." *Bulletin of Christian Institutes of Islamic Studies* 4 (2), 98–104.

1983. "A Culturally Sensitive Area." *Evangelical Review of Theology* 7 (2): 274–76.

1983. "Applied Spirituality in Ministry among Muslims." *Missiology* 11 (4): 435–47.

1983. *Bridges to Islam.* Grand Rapids: Baker.

1985. *Beyond the Mosque: Christians within Muslim Community.* Grand Rapids: Baker.

1985. "How to Change Medicine to Muslims." *Evangelical Missions Quarterly* 21 (3), 253–55.

1987. "How Spiritual Are Missionaries?" *Evangelical Missions Quarterly* 23 (1): 8–16.

1989. "Lessons Learned in Contextualization." In *Muslims and Christians on the Emmaus Road*, edited by Dudley Woodberry, 251–65. Monrovia, CA: Missions Advanced Research.

1989. *The Cross and the Crescent.* Carol Stream, IL: Tyndale.

1990. "Why Some People Are Unproductive." *Evangelical Missions Quarterly* 26 (3): 251–53.

1994. *Inside the Community.* Grand Rapids: Baker.

1994. "Missionaries: Safe or Expendable?" *Evangelical Missions Quarterly* 30 (2): 162–66.

1994. *Understanding Muslim Teachings and Traditions.* Grand Rapids: Baker.

1996. "The Nearest in Affection: Towards a Christian Understanding of Islam." *International Bulletin of Missionary Research* 20 (2): 86.

1998. "Danger! New Directions in Contextualization." *Evangelical Missions Quarterly* 34 (4): 404–6, 409–10.

1998. "Other Options for Muslim Evangelism." *Evangelical Missions Quarterly* 34 (1): 38–42.

2000. *Divine Threads within a Human Tapestry: Memoirs of Phil Parshall.* Pasadena, CA: William Carey Library.

2000. *The Last Great Frontier.* Quezon City, Philippines: Open Doors.

2001. "Muslim Evangelism: Mobilizing the National Church." *Evangelical Missions Quarterly* 37 (1): 44–47.

2002. *The Cross and the Crescent.* Downers Grove, IL: InterVarsity.

2003. *Muslim Evangelism: Contemporary Approaches to Contextualization.* Waynesboro: GA: Gabriel Publishing.

2004. "Lifting the Fatwa." *Evangelical Missions Quarterly* 40 (3): 288–93.

2007. *Muslim Evangelism: Contemporary Approaches to Contextualization.* Colorado Springs, CO: Biblica.

2012. "Contextualization." In *Toward Respectful Understanding and Witness among Muslims: Essays in Honor of J. Dudley Woodberry,* edited by E. Reisacher. Pasadena, CA: William Carey Library.

2013. "Too Much Context May Harm: I Learned the Limits in Contextualizing the Gospel for Muslims." *Christianity Today* 57 (1): 21.

ALSO FROM
WILLIAM CAREY PUBLISHING

Calling on the Prophets: In Christian Witness to Muslims
Colin Bearup

Clues to Africa, Islam, and the Gospel: Insights for New Workers
Colin Bearup

Fruit to Harvest: Witness of God's Great Work among Muslims
Gene Daniels, Pam Arlund, and Jim Heney, editors

Honor, Shame, and the Gospel: Reframing Our Message and Ministry
Christopher Flanders and Werner Mischke, editors

Insider Church: Ekklesia and the Insider Paradigm
S. T. Antonio

Margins of Islam: Ministry in Diverse Muslim Contexts
Gene Daniels and Wes Watkins, editors

Available at missionbooks.org